Preservation & Building Codes

Papers from the Preservation and Building Codes conference, sponsored by the National Trust for Historic Preservation, Washington, D.C., May 1974.

COSPONSORED BY:

Advisory Council on Historic Preservation
American Institute of Architects
American Insurance Association
Association for Preservation Technology
Building Officials and Code Administrators, International
International Conference of Building Officials
National Conference of State Historic Preservation Officers
National Fire Protection Association
National Register of Historic Places, National Park Service
Society of Architectural Historians, Preservation Committee
Southern Building Code Congress

Published by:
THE PRESERVATION PRESS,
NATIONAL TRUST FOR HISTORIC PRESERVATION
IN THE UNITED STATES

THE PRESERVATION PRESS — 1975
National Trust for Historic Preservation
740-748 Jackson Place, N.W.
Washington, D.C. 20006

Printed in the United States of America.
Library of Congress Catalogue Card Number 75-21153
ISBN 0-89133-035-6

The National Trust for Historic Preservation, chartered by Congress in 1949, is the only private, nonprofit organization with the responsibility to encourage public participation in the preservation of sites, buildings and objects significant in American history and culture. Support is provided by membership dues, endowment funds and contributions and by matching grants from the U.S. Department of the Interior, National Park Service, under provisions of the National Historic Preservation Act of 1966.

The conference was planned by Russell V. Keune, AIA, director, Peter H. Smith, assistant director, and Baird M. Smith of the Department of Field Services of the National Trust. The conference was conducted with the aid of Theresa M. Profilet and Samuel G. Welsh of the Trust. The National Trust expresses appreciation to the Northern Virginia Park Authority and to J. Everette Fauber, Jr., and associates, architects, for arranging the tour of preservation projects in Old Town, Alexandria, Va. The proceedings were edited by Jennie B. Bull, associate editor, The Preservation Press.

Cover art: Architectural drawings for restoration of Gadsby's Tavern, Alexandria, Va. First floor miscellaneous details. (J. Everette Fauber, Jr. FAIA)

Contents

Foreword

Building codes play a pivotal role in the retention of our architectural heritage. The National Trust is thus pleased to have organized the first national conference on historic preservation and building codes. The program was another of the recent National Trust technical conferences focusing on special preservation issues of national interest—1971, preservation law; 1972, historic districts; 1973, urban landmark commissions.

There is no question that public and private interest in identifying, evaluating, protecting, preserving and using our nation's rich heritage of architectural resources is increasingly widespread. The present economy and the energy shortages have made recycling existing buildings even more necessary, and the National Trust believes this commitment to preservation will grow at an even greater pace during the nation's Bicentennial celebration.

The Trust was particularly encouraged by the responses received from the major national code organizations represented by speakers on the program.

As a result of the increase in private and public funds available for historic preservation, the number of inquiries coming to the National Trust on code-related matters has increased substantially. Material containing various references to the development of the Building Officials and Code Administrators statewide building code started to come through the Field Services Department of the Trust in 1972. The department began to alert Trust members and in particular state historic preservation officers when it knew procedures were under way to begin development of statewide building codes with provisions for historic buildings. The Southern Building Codes Conference asked the Trust for aid in preparation of material for its magazine. This was perhaps the first major step toward communication. Then the historic preservation amendment to the BOCA code began to be considered. A Trust representative appeared in public testimony at the BOCA hearing in Fort Lauderdale in January 1974. This was the first time the Trust undertook public testimony about building codes. The plan to organize this conference grew directly out of that effort.

A few words on how the conference was structured are in order. Participants began with a look at what constitutes a historic resource and moved on to an overview of some current issues faced by architects in their past and current preservation projects. Three studies of how the preservationist and the code official developed means to resolve issues furnished examples for others to consider for applicability to their own situations. Presentations by representatives of the code organizations provided an indication of their respective viewpoints toward specific areas of interest. An evening tour focused on building code considerations with three ongoing preservation projects in Old Town Alexandria, Va. The conference concluded with a look toward the future from the viewpoint of national representatives and in two conference summaries, one representing the viewpoint of code officials and the other the preservationist viewpoint.

The National Trust looks forward to continued sponsorship of national technical conferences and is encouraged by activities both within and outside the organization that have followed from some of its past conferences. It is hoped that at some time in the future we can look back to this conference as a point at which the objectives of preservation and building codes assumed a new relationship.

James Biddle, president
National Trust for Historic Preservation

Defining a Historic Building and District

WILLIAM J. MURTAGH

William J. Murtagh is keeper of the National Register of Historic Places. He was formerly assistant to the president and director of education and of program with the National Trust for Historic Preservation.

The answer to the question of what constitutes a historic building or district is the basic problem facing many groups that attempt to deal with the problem of changing the existing environment. It is the difference in conceptualization of this definition that lays the basis for the common local controversy over whether a building stays or goes, or indeed, whether a neighborhood stabilizes or devours itself to metamorphose into a different state.

Webster's Seventh New Collegiate Dictionary defines a building as "a usually roofed and walled structure built for permanent use (as for a dwelling)." On the basis of this definition, a corrugated tin garage can be accepted as a building, as can The Breakers, the Vanderbilt family "cottage" by the sea in Newport, R.I. Distinctions creep into such comparisons when one considers how the building is put together structurally and how it is conceived stylistically and spatially. It follows that the application of aesthetic intellect to the building process produces more than just a building, but a creation that either pleases or displeases according to how successful and sensitive its creator has been in understanding the taste of the day and its abstracts of compatibility. Thus, the builder who has the intellectual capacity and informed knowledge to conceptualize and produce an aesthetically acceptable product is called an architect, and the method of intellectualizing the combination of materials and spaces to produce this positive end result, architecture, is an art form no different from that of a painting, a statue, a musical composition, a city plan or a well-cut suit, save in the materials used.

All artistic endeavor demands a sensitivity to the abstracts of form, color, texture, material, etc., to produce an artistic product. The failure to evaluate such abstracts as products of their age, by evaluating them instead on the basis of current taste standards, generates calloused attitudes toward the existing cultural environment. Thus, the throw-away mentality of the 20th-century plastic world often finds craftsmanship and artistic sensitivity difficult to accept and harder still to understand and appreciate.

Interior view of New York Shakespeare Festival Public Theater. (George Cserna)

If we accept a building on which artistic intellect has been lavished as evidence that architecture is a fine art, then what is a "historic building?" Traditionally, Americans have demanded that such a building have some association with events or lives of persons who have made significant contributions to history. It thus follows that unless such associations can be documented the building is not historic. Simple solution: Tear it down.

Attitudes and philosophies of this nature were perfectly acceptable as long as Americans confined the definition of *heritage* to a landmark building, intellectually isolated from its environment, the historicity of which was unassailable by documentation through association with the person who lived there or events that took place there. Mount Vernon and Independence Hall are two obvious examples of buildings preservable for their associative values alone.

In 1931 a new concept dawned upon the United States when the city of Charleston, S.C., decided, with the general public benefit in mind, to restrict to a further degree than ever before in this country the ability of the private citizen to change his own property within a certain neighborhood. This intensification of the police power, through selective local zoning of The Battery, spawned many such other areas, referred to in this country as historic districts, and gave rise to the necessity to develop new attitudes and definitions of preservation as a form of city planning. Into the roux of historicity have thus been stirred architectonic excellence, spatial relationships and street furniture, among others. Out of this matrix has developed our current concern for that which the French call ambiental preservation, the British, conservation areas, and the Americans, old and historic districts.

Turning to *Webster's Unabridged*, we note that it defines a district as "territorial division (as of a nation, state, county, or city) marked off or defined for administrative, electoral, judicial, or other purposes." Thus, in the context of the viable city, the museum landmark building is but one pivotal unit in a linkage of units that collectively define the walls of continuity of a street space. To this are added the textural qualities of the surface materials and those built and natural elements collectively known as street furniture, such as trees, shrubs, directional signs, trash receptacles, lamps, etc. In total, the manner in which these elements combine renders an impact on the consciousness of the beholder that orients the sensibilities, directing the viewer to mentally conclude that the location or neighborhood is of distinct specificity. Thus, neighborhoods having that indefinable quality called character communicate visually through this sense of locality, which is real and readily perceptible. This specificity of locality arises from the ease of recognition of the boundaries of the neighborhood, the design or style of the buildings, the materials of which they are constructed, the way they relate to each other spatially, the quality of their workmanship and, perhaps, their associative values, in addition to the coordinated design quality of the street furniture.

Every such fully developed district contains a series of focal or pivotal buildings that form the framework of the urban fabric. These are usually, but not necessarily, public structures. This framework is supported by linkages of less important structures without which the pivotal buildings exist only as isolated entities. Collectively, however, with the spaces between them, the streets and sidewalks, as well as the street furniture, they produce a total identity of place. Whether the units are individually restored or not is peripheral to the question, providing the total sense of identity is present. Thus, the sum total of the parts exceeds in value any of its individual units, yet the recognition of the value of each of the contributors (e.g., the spaces, the street furniture and the original architectonic value of the individual buildings), irrespective of their quality, produces an identity and specificity of time and place. It follows, therefore, that the introduction of concrete sidewalks and steel-pole cold-cathode street lights inevitably erodes this sense of time and place in a neighborhood that developed at a period when brick sidewalks were used and cast-iron-supported gas lamps were current. In like manner, Bricktex, aluminum siding and asbestos shingling have a similar deteriorating effect in neighborhoods where such materials are alien to those originally used. Authenticity in materials is of prime importance on street facades in urban settings, since this is usually the only portion of a building that makes a contribution to the streetscape and becomes one of the contributors to this sense of locality.

The quality of locality or neighborhood identity erodes in direct proportion to the increasing number of nonconforming intrusions that change the sense of place. Thus, the destruction of a single building in a row changes the delicate spatial relationship of the individual units to each other and to the streetscape by eroding the closed sense of the defining wall of continuity. Similarly, the insertion of new buildings out of character in scale, proportion, materials, texture, color, etc., with existing adjacent structures has an equivalent deteriorating effect. The acrylics of the 20th-century gas station and the 20th-century spatial arrangement usually accepted pro forma as necessary for its function likewise depress the physiological and visual quality of a traditional neighborhood. This is not to say that new buildings and new functions have no place in the neighborhoods of the average older urban American environment, but the design problems of integrating these changed neighborhood functions have never been addressed on a large scale in this country.

In conclusion, it should be restated that these comments are made in the context of the operable urban fabric. Thus, all other considerations aside, the individual "historic" house has validity for preservation on the basis of those aesthetic qualities that reflect the age of its creation. If it happens to have associative values with important persons or events, so much the better, despite the fact that these are not necessarily a determinant of its contribution to the American heritage. Even these aesthetic qualities may individually be far less striking when the anonymous units of a linkage of buildings are considered in the context of a district. Indeed, in such district situations associative values can play nonexistent or minimum roles. The acceptability of aesthetics or impact on human consciousness in preference to associative values is, of course, the basis now for the recognition of preservation as a special form of city planning, especially in districts where the cultural ecology of the nation becomes the preeminent concern of the environmental issue. Thus, when the Charleston district ordinance launched the new planning directions in preservation in this country, concern for the national patrimony was no longer the exclusive purview of the curator and social-intellectual historian concerned for the single educational entity—the historic house museum. As we enter the final quarter of the 20th century, the legacy we strive to leave for future generations is a concept of a quality of life. This is born of necessity and the recognition that existing nonrenewable built resources hold in large part the answer to the search for the stability that we seek in a highly mobile age. It is mandatory that this philosophy become a part of the average American consciousness as a necessity of life, rather than an elective.

Discussion

Comments made by William J. Murtagh and the audience during the discussion following presentation of his paper are here summarized.

The restored and adapted historic house museum can be regarded as an educational tool. It is no different in its teaching potential from a written history text, except in dimension. One walks through the space instead of sitting down with a book and reading the history of the building.

The value judgments applied to the historic house museum are determined by the educational experience one expects the building to convey. If the building's purpose is to relate the story of a single person or family or of a certain period in time in a certain place in our country, then one can rightly ignore other periods that have no role to play in the interpretation of the building. However, if there is no pivotal figure who can function as the fulcrum around which the associative values revolve, then it seems questionable to ignore later periods. Restoration span depends on the message being conveyed.

The associative values of anonymous structures in historic districts are, for the most part, either minimal or nonexistent. For structures in historic districts the term *restoration*, which is loosely applied to such efforts, is better replaced by the term *rehabilitation*. The term *restoration* generally applies only to the street facade, and then only if a good job is done. In rehabilitation, the basic criterion is bringing the building, especially the interior, up to 20th-century demands of comfortable living. If additions to the structure add to that quotient of comfortable living, then there is justification for leaving whatever addition is there.

However, there are differences of opinion concerning new construction in historic districts. For instance, the historic district Georgetown, D.C., is reflective of the past bleakness of the local preservation law and the narrowness of attitudes of past review board representatives in interpreting what was acceptable new architecture in relationship to the historic structures. The Georgetown preservation legislation and its interpretation prevented, until very recently, good contemporary architecture. But it did not prevent a home owner from creating a 20th-century anomaly from a good late-19th-century unit by stripping characteristics of its age and applying modern elements to the front. The excellently designed townhouse on the east side of Georgetown in Washington, by Hugh N. Jacobson, AIA, is an outstanding example of contemporary architecture functioning successfully in the traditional settled neighborhood. Contemporary architecture should by all means be acceptable in a historic neighborhood, but it is a sad fact that the average American architect is far from capable of successfully confronting this difficult design problem.

Current Issues

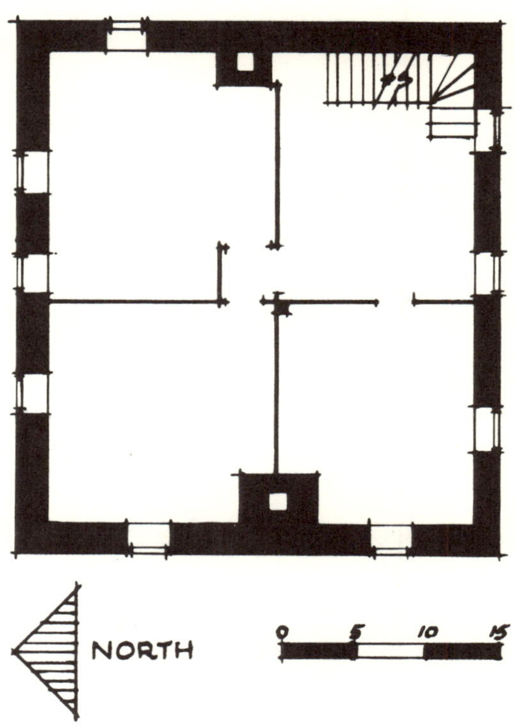
NORTH
0
5
10
15

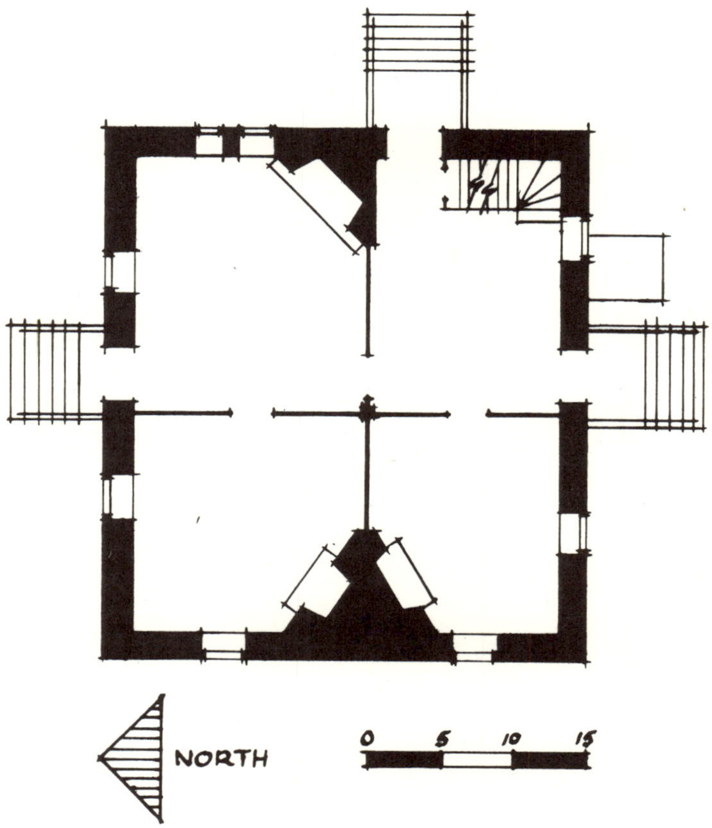
NORTH
0
5
10
15

Small-Scale Preservation Projects

ORIN M. BULLOCK, JR., FAIA

Orin M. Bullock, Jr., FAIA, is a practicing architect in Baltimore, Md. Since 1967 his practice has been restricted to the restoration of historic buildings as a consultant or as principal architect. He is the author of The Restoration Manual.

This paper deals with small restoration projects and the effects that strict compliance with the building codes has, or might have had, on the authenticity of the finished work. Problems differ with each building, with a determination of the degree the historical significance of the building would suffer and with an evaluation of the hazard to public health and safety that might result from modification or relaxation of code requirements.

In each project selected for this review there was an attempt to preserve the architectural integrity of the building, and the only alteration in building use was to make each available for public visitation. To a greater or lesser degree, all fail to comply with the literal requirements of some of the building codes, particularly as related to materials, construction and exitways.

Buildings are preserved and restored in order to retain important elements of the historical and architectural heritage. One measure of the success of preservation projects is the accuracy with which the monuments present the space, the architectural features and the atmosphere of the period that is represented. Strict compliance with contemporary codes and ordinances related to buildings used for public occupancy would in many cases result in violent intrusion on the historic atmosphere to be preserved. In order to fully achieve this purpose, a historic building must be open for visitation and use by the public. This use places the restorationist on the horns of a dilemma, for public safety, health and welfare must be insured.

Perhaps the most serious problems are caused by intrusions and modifications necessary to provide acceptable means of egress. Often, open stairways must be enclosed, additional flights added, winders removed or abandoned, exits widened and doorway swings reversed.

HEZEKIAH ALEXANDER HOUSE *(c. 1774), Charlotte, N.C. First floor plan (above); second floor plan (below). (Orin M. Bullock, Jr., FAIA)*

Structural systems cannot always be strengthened, nor successfully fire-stopped, nor can old single-board partitions be made fire resistant.

A reasonable relaxation of a literal application of the codes and acceptable regulations delimiting allowable uses must be formulated for each project with the building officials concerned. The same sorts of problems, but with varying degrees of magnitude, occurred in each of the examples discussed in this paper.

One that is as vital to use as well as to safety involves the circulation, which is essential to the orderly showing of a small domestic building: in some cases the addition of a new stair may be possible and may solve the problem of use as well as safety. Such a solution solved both problems in Philipsburg Manor, Tarrytown, N.Y., where a "required stair" was installed with no damage to the atmosphere or the historic character of the house.

Since most problems in preservation projects caused by the codes relate to the possibility of fire, the most obvious diminution of the problem is to prohibit all smoking and open flames in the building. Safety officials will sometimes relax exit requirements if it can be shown that major hazards can be eliminated.

HEZEKIAH ALEXANDER HOUSE

A two-story stone house in Mecklenburg County, near Charlotte, N.C., was built in 1774 by Hezekiah Alexander, a signer of the Mecklenburg Declaration of Independence in 1755. It has been restored with unusual care to its original appearance by the Hezekiah Alexander Restoration Foundation, on the basis of extant physical evidence and exhaustive historical research. It is to be opened to the public as a house museum. Located on an open site, the house and outbuildings are more than 300 yards from the nearest structures.

Description

The house has two stories with a basement and attic, built of substantial random rubble stone exterior walls plastered directly on the inside. The floors are carried on a wood post, girder and exposed joist system. The soffits of all floors, which are of single thickness, are exposed. All interior partitions are of 1-inch cypress vertical board paneling, except the one in the basement, which is of stone. A narrow winding stair provides the only access to the second floor and to the attic; access to the basement is provided by a flight under the winding stair and by a bulkhead stair to the front. The house has three rooms in the basement, four on each floor and one in the attic. Adequate exitways from the first floor are provided by doors on the front and rear and at one end.

The subject of access to the upper floors is the basic question. How many persons constitute a public assembly? It is doubtful that this building will be normally filled to capacity on the basis of room sizes, but any group circulation pattern will be difficult, no matter how it is done, if a tour is to include the entire house, the basement and the attic.

The winding stair is typical of houses of the period, from Pennsylvania to the Carolinas. It is not comfortable to use, and only agile young people will go up and down at anything but a snail's pace. It has been provided with a handrail so that a person may grasp something when taking a step, but winding stairs are outlawed by current building codes as a means of access or egress.

Climate control is provided by dual electrical systems, one in the attic and one in the basement. For the first floor, air is introduced through ducts buried in the great stone chimneys at both ends of the building, and for the second floor it is brought through peripheral ceiling slots. Air returns to the basement unit through the fireplaces and to the attic unit up the attic stair; the second floor door to the attic must be kept ajar. The fireplaces have been made inoperable.

Illumination is provided by high-intensity lamps, dimmer controlled and mounted on the sides of the floor joists. Electric service is connected to the building underground; the panel and mechanical equipment occupy an enclosed space in the basement.

Fire and burglar alarms are connected with the fire and police departments. The building is roofed with C-rated, fire-retardant-dipped, hand-split shingles. Plumbing vents are concealed in a chimney.

Critical Effects of Code Requirements

The design and structural integrity of the interior would be lost if the partition walls and floor system were altered to provide the fire resistance required in buildings used for public assembly. A historically unacceptable modification of the winding stairs would be required to meet exit standards. The provision of an unobtrusive return of controlled air from the second floor was technically impossible other than by the utilization of the stair to the attic.

Less Critical Neglect of Code Requirements

Only one toilet facility is provided.

Doors to the exterior open inward.

Doors enclosing the stairs are located three risers above the floor.

There is only one exit from the second floor (the winding stair).

Exits are not identified by signs.

Rationale for Variances from Codes

The number of persons admitted to the house at any one time will be less than the number normally considered a public assembly. Other than on the first floor and in the basement, where the exits are adequate, the arrangement of the house is not conducive to showing it to large numbers of persons consecutively.

Even though the interior is not fireproof or even fire resistant, no open flames are to be allowed in the building: therefore only a minimum fire hazard exists.

Meeting House of the Society of Friends

The Old Friends Meeting House, Newport, R.I., was restored to its appearance during the period from 1699 to 1858. The historical integrity of the original building and two major additions made during that period are being preserved. The meeting house became so popular as a meeting place for the Society of Friends in the later part of the 19th century that additions were found necessary in 1857 and in 1875, designed to conform with the architectural taste of those periods. These radical changes altered the appearance of the building, destroying or concealing now rare architectural features. The goal of the project was to restore as much as possible of the structure's early architectural history.

A gift from the family of Sydney L. Wright to the Newport Historical Society, it is open to the public and for meetings of the Society of Friends. The building stands on the east side of a 2½-acre plot fronting on two streets. The nearest buildings are two frame dwellings about 40 feet to the east and a masonry building about 30 feet to the south.

Description

All three sections of the wood building, which rests on a rock and rubble stone foundation, are of heavy post and girder, braced frame construction. The Great Meeting (center section), which was started in 1699, is medieval in character, with the massive framing exposed on the interior. The section is 45 feet square, 21 feet from the floor to the roof plate and open from the floor to the cupola surmounting the pyramidical roof, which was obscured only by wall-to-wall girders that are still in place. The exterior walls are enclosed with heavy oak planks running from sill to plate, shingled or clapboarded on the exterior and lathed and plastered between the framing members on the interior. There is a balcony, with a plastered soffit, around three sides of the room.

The section to the north, 35 by 45 feet, was built in 1730. It is similarly framed and finished, except that the framing members are cased and there is a second floor. The ceilings on both floors are plastered.

The section to the south, 45 feet square, was built in 1807, and the great hipped roof of the first building was lowered at that time. This section has stud walls, lathed and plastered between an exposed cased-post and girder framing system. It is shingled on the exterior with horizontal sheathing. The section is open the full two stories, has a plastered ceiling and once had a balcony, which also had a plastered soffit, around three sides. The portion at the west end is original.

The exterior door of the Great Meeting is 6 feet wide. The North Meeting has a 4-foot-wide exterior door through a vestibule door of the same size and, in addition, a 2 foot 6 inch door at the foot of the stair to the second floor. The South Meeting has two exterior doors, each 6 feet wide. Only the doors in the North Meeting open out.

The three sections open into one another at the ground floor if movable partitions are raised. When the partitions are closed, wicket doors provide passage. The second floor of the North Meeting is connected to the balcony of the Great Meeting by a 30-inch-wide door.

The building is equipped with smoke and fire detectors and alarms that are connected with the fire and police departments. There is no central heating system; an electric unit in the basement toilet room maintains the temperature above freezing. Use of the fireplace and stove, served by the chimney in the North Meeting, will be restricted. The roof is covered with C-rated, fire-retardant wood shingles. Plumbing vents are carried a considerable distance under the floor and concealed in the chimney. Electric service is connected to the building underground; meters and panels are concealed in a cabinet in the wall of the north vestibule.

Critical Effects of Code Requirements

Unless exceptions are made permitting the use of an entirely nonfireproof building, there could be no restoration of such a monument.

Because of the presence of exterior shutter doors as well as security doors, only the doors from the north wing could be opened out without a radical departure from documented appearance.

Rationale for Variances from Codes

Visitation to the building will be by small, controlled groups that will tour with escorts. When seated assemblies are held, the number of persons will be restricted, and the in-swinging doors, of which there are an ample number that are well located of suitable size, will be secured in an open position. The intent of the law will be fulfilled by insuring that the doors are kept open in the event of a public assembly. Another option is to cut the strap hinges on the doors that open in, supply butts and allow the doors to open out. The butts separate the hinges as a door swings open, so that when a door is open the paths of the strap hinges are visible. This would be disconcerting to historical-minded visitors.

The absence of open flames and smoking in the building reduces the hazard of an internally ignited fire. There are a minimum number of lighting fixtures, and all wiring conforms to code requirements.

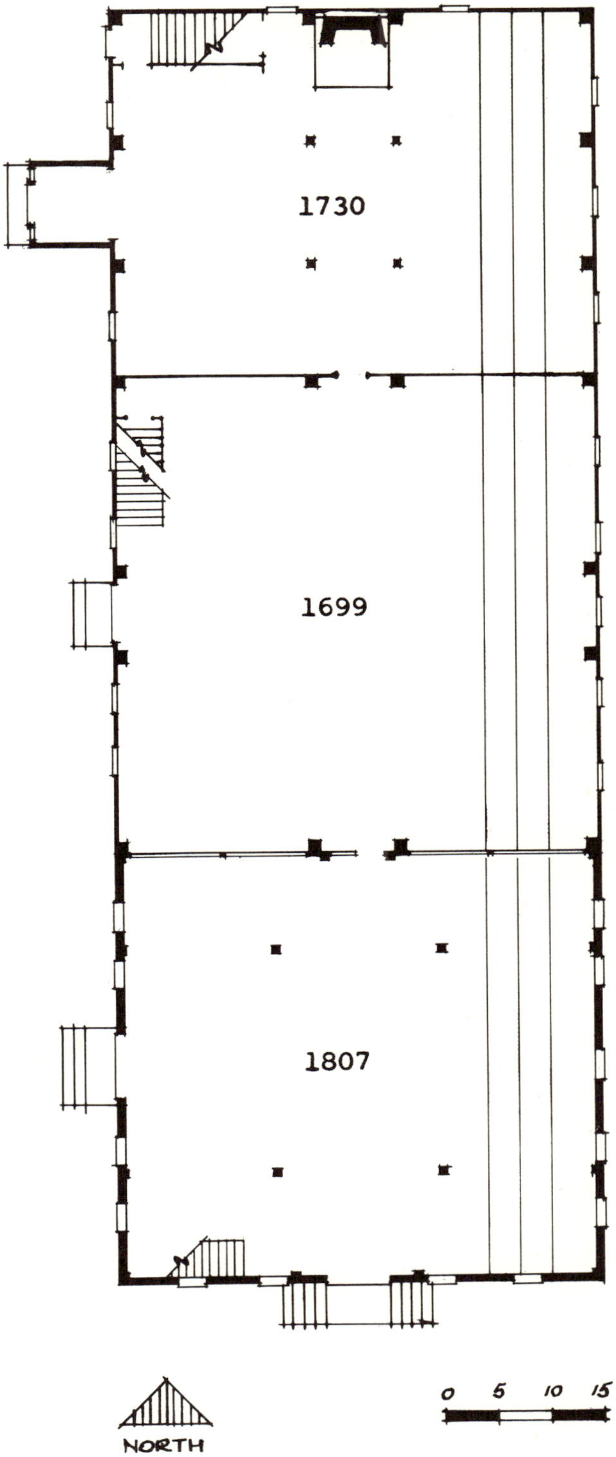

Society of Friends Meeting House, *Newport, R.I. Ground floor plan. (Bullock)*

Fire and police department headquarters are within two blocks of the building.

Tudor Hall

Tudor Hall, a brick, two-story house, was built in the 18th century, completely modified and enlarged in the early 19th century and converted into a county library in the early 20th century. It is located in Leonardtown, St. Mary's County, Md., and is owned by the county. It was restored and improved during 1972 and 1973 with the aid of a U.S. Department of Housing and Urban Development grant for continued use as a public library. The program for this project called for adaptive use and the retention of all possible original work, a goal not unlike that currently guiding the Society for the Preservation of New England Antiquities. The structure was run-down and has been refurbished, not restored, retaining everything possible from the 19th-century work.

Description

The building is a long, rectangular, hip-roofed structure, 90 by 30 feet, built on a high, wooded site of slightly more than one acre, overlooking Bretton Bay, one block from the center of Leonardtown.

The exterior walls and the two transverse walls carrying the chimneys are of brick; all other interior partitions are of wood, lath and plaster. The floor construction is of wood and the ceilings are plastered.

The basement accommodates a reading room, a stack room, a boiler room and toilet facilities. Egress is provided at each end of the floor.

The ground floor accommodates a reading room, the circulation room, two workrooms and a juvenile room. Egress is provided on all four sides in five locations by stoops or porches to grade. The original front and back doors open in and are not marked as exits.

The second floor accommodates an adult reading room, an adult fiction stack room, a music room, a special collection room, toilet facilities, a staff lounge and the librarian's office. Egress is provided at both ends of the building.

The original stair, which is not enclosed, ascends from the front entrance door at the circulation room to the second floor hall at the music room.

A dumbwaiter has been installed to transport books to all three floors.

A fire detection system is connected to the civil defense headquarters one block away.

Critical Effects of Code Requirements

Plumbing vents have been carried through the roof surface, providing a visible reminder of the presence of fixtures below.

Plan integrity was sacrificed on the first and second floors to provide space in the northwest corner for the fire stair.

A normally mandatory ramp, which would have detracted from the historical integrity of the exterior, was not required because another county library, built at grade level, is available for paraplegics.

This is a building that succeeds in most ways, but, as usual, fails in a few other ways.

TUDOR HALL *(c. 1850), Leonardtown, Md. First floor plan. (Bullock)*

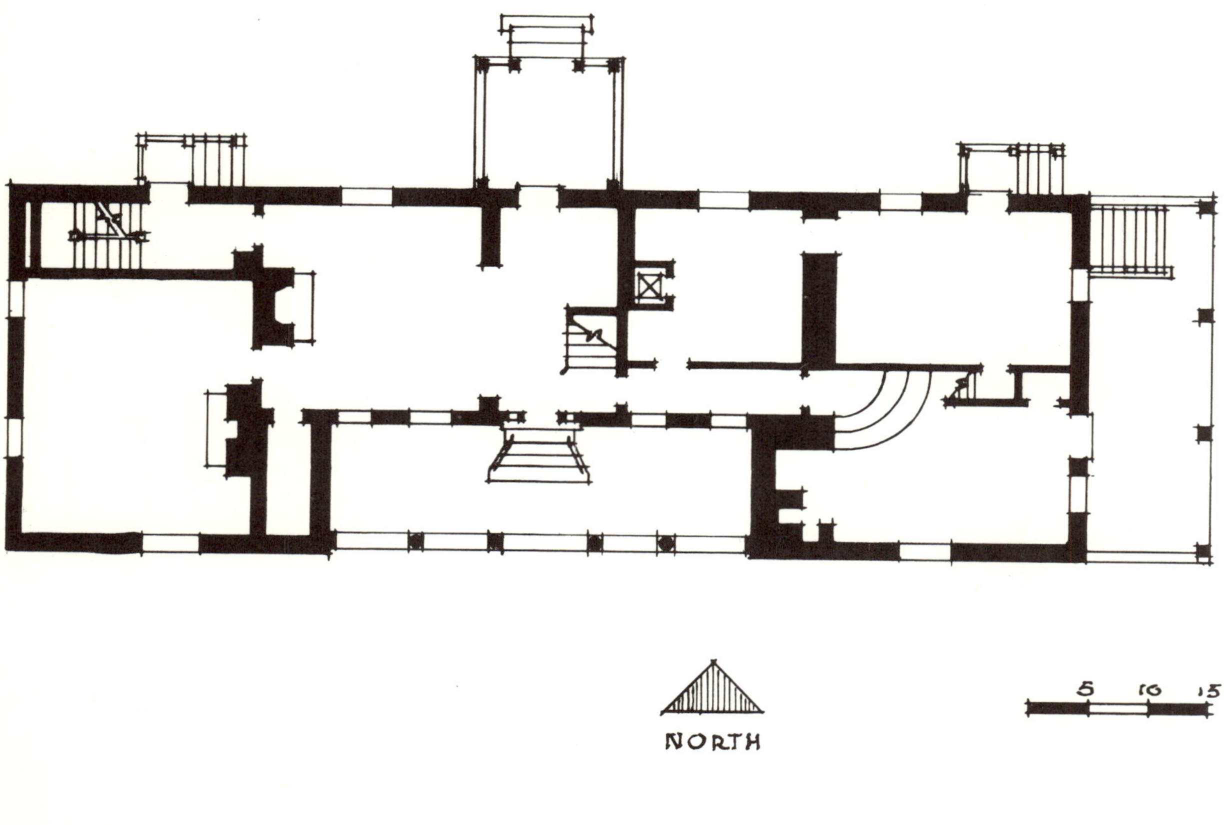

Panic hardware was provided only on the required exits, where its presence does not detract noticeably from the historical character of the building.

Required exit signs were provided and, wherever possible, doors were omitted from the openings along exitways, a compromise with historical integrity.

Old Colony House

The first state house for Rhode Island (completed c. 1740) stands at the head of Washington Square in Newport with a view to Narragansett Bay. In about 1918 Norman Isham, an architect and well-known early preservationist, directed a major restoration of the building. Since that time it has been open to the public as a historical exhibit. It is not regularly used as a place of public assembly. Old Colony House is currently being studied, and more accurate restoration of many of its features is being considered by the state.

Description

The two-story building is built of brick with a slate roof, over a full basement. The first floor is one large room, approximately 80 feet by 40 feet, with a broad stair ascending to the second floor. The only access to the basement is via a stair below the stair to the second floor. The second floor originally contained the Deputies Room, the Middle Room and a Council Room. All have been altered in size and architectural character through the years.

Critical Effects of Code Requirements

The entire structural system is of wood except for the exterior walls.

Two of the three exits, double value doors, swing in. The west door, the main entrance, has been rehung to open out on butt hinges, but strap hinge plates remain on the inside and resemble the original hardware when the door is closed.

The stairway to the second floor is about 48 inches wide and is open from the first floor to a door on the flight of stairs from the second floor to the attic. There is no secondary egress from the second floor or from the attic, in which there are two rooms not open to the public. The use of these rooms might be a violation of the law since there is only one means of egress, which is in itself inadequate.

No panic hardware has been provided, and no exit signs or directions have been provided.

Rationale for Variances from Codes

Normal use is by small groups of visitors conducted by a guide. When occasional assemblies are held, special precautions are taken to insure unobstructed egress through the doors.

Old Colony House *(c. 1740), Newport, R.I. Second floor plan. (Bullock)*

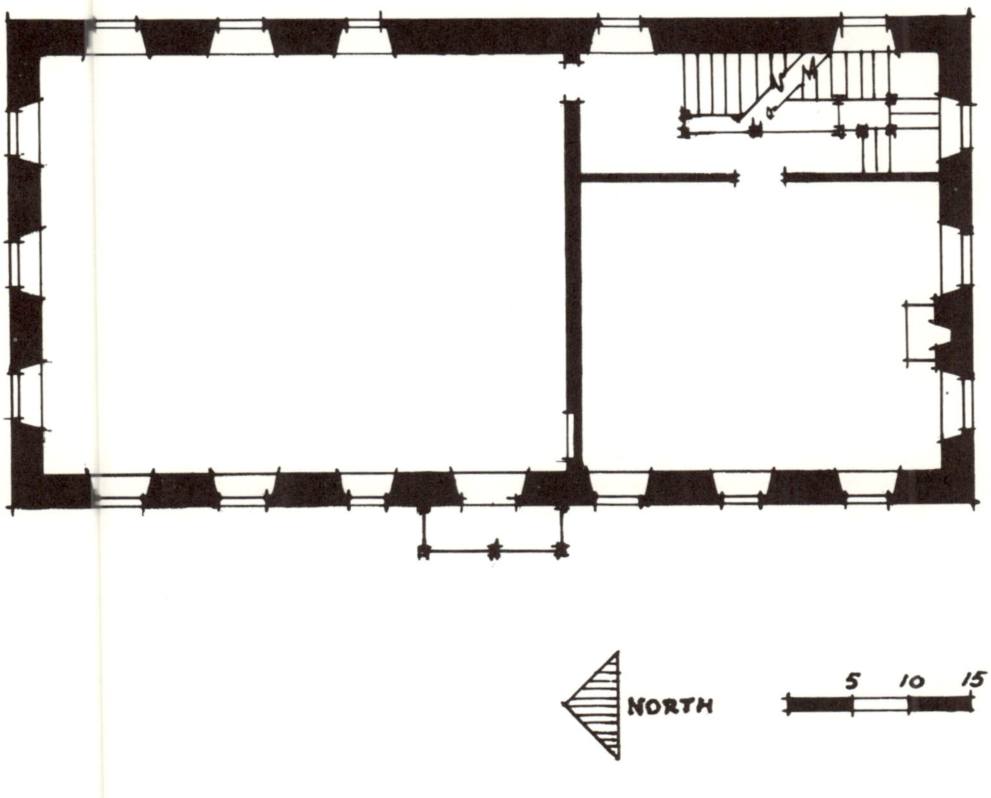

Summary

The effects of strict compliance to building codes are relative, depending first on the size, location, construction system and original layout of a historic building and second on the determination of use, anticipated occupancy and classification as established by the designated building official.

The Occupational Safety and Health Administration (OSHA) code, adopted by Congress and in effect since April 28, 1971, if literally followed would restrict the public presentation of many historic buildings and prevent the authentic restoration of others. Other codes, such as those of the National Board of Fire Underwriters and the Building Officials & Code Administrators (BOCA), are equally specific but do not have the overall authority of federal law.

For example, Title 29—Labor, Chapter XVII, OSHA, Subpart E—Means of Egress, Section 1910.36 (b) Fundamental requirements. (1) states:

> Every building or structure, new or old, designed for human occupancy shall be provided with exits sufficient to permit the prompt escape of occupants in case of fire or other emergency. The design of exits and other safeguards shall be such that reliance for safety in case of fire or other emergency will not depend solely on any single safeguard; additional safeguards shall be provided for life safety in case any single safeguard is ineffective due to some human or mechanical failure.

Section 1910.37—Means of Egress, General, (a) Permissible components, also states: "An exit shall consist only of the approved components. Exit components shall be constructed as an integral part of the building or shall be permanently affixed thereto."

The code continues, to describe in detail the requirements for fire separation, automatic closing doors, widths and capacities of means of egress, ramps and levels, numbers and separation of exits, etc.

Fire safety code requirements are numerous and specific and include fire-resistant separation of spaces (such as firestops within a structure), the prohibition of winders in stairs and noncombustible construction of stairs throughout. All of these requirements are geared to establishment of an occupancy classification, but I have not found a definition of the smallest number of persons who shall constitute a public assembly. No fire marshal or fire engineer will approve and take the responsiiblity for what he considers to be a major nonconforming proposal or use unless it can be shown that hazards have been otherwise minimized, and many are strictly "by the book" men.

Structural code requirements, such as those concerning natural light and ventilation, clearance in crawl spaces, loading, plumbing, heating and electrical work, can be met in almost all cases without material damage to small restoration projects.

The purpose of selecting this group of museum quality buildings for discussion was to illustrate some of the variations that make the literal application of the regulations relating to fire protection almost impossible if an authentic restoration is to be achieved. Each restoration project is an individual problem that must be solved through a careful weighing of values and hazards endemic in most old buildings if they are to be preserved for public use retaining original work. Solutions in each case must include all possible measures to minimize possible hazards and provide safe means of escape for visitor occupants and still retain the architectural features that warrant the preservation of the structure.

Large-Scale Preservation Projects

GIORGIO CAVAGLIERI, FAIA

Giorgio Cavaglieri, FAIA, is a practicing architect in New York City specializing in restoration and adaptive use of urban public structures.

Large-scale preservation projects in urban communities presuppose the existence of groups of buildings that possess historic or architectural features of landmark quality around which new construction and new facilities have been erected.

It is likely that the grounds that surround these buildings, including the roads and open space, have undergone such transformations that the preservation of the historic character of the area is almost impossible. Sidewalks, paving materials, trees, grass paths, street furniture and so on either have disappeared over the years or have been so thoroughly changed that the impact of the original environment has been lost.

Because of new habits and technological developments changes occur in the utilities (water supply, electricity and electric cables, telephone and gas lines, etc.) and this results in continuous digging and closing of open area surfaces. Eventually nothing is left of the original design of the approaches to the buildings and the general character of the environment. With the possible exception, therefore, of a luxury mansion isolated in a park, a large-scale preservation project is simply the protection and development of separate, individual buildings with the sum presented in a suitable framework. The preservation of the space between the buildings provides a visual reconstruction or interpretation recreated from historical designs of the past.

The problem of code enforcement in relation to the adaptive reuse of existing historic buildings is one of the most easily misunderstood parts of an already difficult field.

Most people who are unfamiliar with the labyrinth of urban life believe that the difficulties of preserving an old building are primarily financial or philosophical in nature. They assume, therefore, that if and when funds for preservation are obtained and a public or a private group is convinced of the aesthetic or historical value of a building, work can proceed speedily and restoration and preservation are assured. Unfortunately, this is not the case. Most urban building codes are written to define the construction of new buildings. Most codes that restrict building materials, uses and construction procedures are studied and written for the protection and safety of the users. Therefore, when an existing building is assigned new purposes or uses, it becomes the responsibility of the authorities to assure the public that the structural and safety characteristics are equal to those of new buildings and are adequate for the new uses.

This adequacy is generally proved by compliance with established regulations. Buildings erected before the regulations were written will in most cases not comply with them. An architect operating in the 1850s could hardly have been expected to foresee the safety provisions and limitations that were to be codified in the 1920s. Moreover, regulations are based on cataloguing and rating the differences among uses; there are different regulations for different uses within a similar enclosure. This situation puzzles the owners or would-be owners of older buildings, and it affects not only their goals but also their pocketbooks.

Roosevelt Island

An interesting example is the case of Roosevelt Island in the East River in New York City. A few hundred feet from the middle of Manhattan and at a subway stop on a line under construction from the busiest commercial center of the city (Bloomingdale's and Alexander's department stores at Lexington Avenue and 60th Street), facilities for a community of 20,000 persons are under construction.

At the beginning of the 19th century, the island was a farm and its few inhabitants commuted to lower Manhattan by ferry or boat. During the middle of the 19th century, several hospitals, some of distinguished design, were built on the island. The hospital personnel and patients constituted a small community living in a semirural atmosphere. As the hospitals became obsolete, some of the buildings were abandoned. They remained in dilapidated condition until it was decided to provide housing facilities on the island.

Seven landmark buildings, varying in area from an 8-foot-diameter lighthouse to a former city hospital of 90,000 square feet, were to be preserved and reused according to the master plan prepared by Philip C. Johnson, FAIA. New uses and activities for restored old buildings designed by James Renwick and Alexander Jackson Davis were intended to complement the residential facilities of this new town. The high-ceilinged spaces and the stone walls of the hospital, when restored for adaptive reuse, would have constituted a relief from the modest appearance of the low-cost housing and the monotony of the highrise apartments, of limited attractiveness even when designed by the most skillful modern architects.

After four years of effort and patient search for a user, the only buildings under restoration are the

almost completed Blackwell House, an 1812 three-bedroom farmhouse, and an 1875 church designed by Frederick Withers, a partner of Calvert Vaux of Central Park fame.

Besides structural restoration, the house needed sprinklers, a ramp and other special facilities for the handicapped, an air-conditioning system and illumination for 50 footcandles at desk height to satisfy the typists intended to occupy it and the requirements for possible federal funds. The stairway had to be completely rebuilt to satisfy the required dimensions of risers and treads, which changed the number of steps.

The church, abandoned when its original Episcopalian congregation dispersed after the City Hospital and the Insane Asylum discontinued operation, was studied for restoration as a religious building to be used by three denominations. In order to obtain approval for occupancy as a church, the building needed windows approximately six times the present size to obtain what the New York State Building Code considers adequate ventilation. Also, new structural reinforcing for the floor was required to permit loading that is considered safe today in a religious building. Ventilation can be provided mechanically rather than with larger windows and structural stability can be obtained with the addition of steel beams. It was difficult, however, for the religious leaders to accept that it would cost the church groups hundreds of

BLACKWELL HOUSE *(1812), Roosevelt Island, New York City. Restored three-bedroom farmhouse. First floor plan (right, above); second floor plan (right, below). (Giorgio Cavaglieri, FAIA)*

thousands of dollars if a public agency were to give back to them the same space in which religious services had been conducted for approximately a century. Because of the cost, use of the building exclusively for religious purposes was impossible and new goals and avenues had to be sought for its preservation.

It was finally decided to convert the church to a community center that would be financed by various organizations and that could be lent occasionally to the religious institutions. However, for this use the anticipated live load had to be increased again and more structural reinforcement added to permit public assembly with movable seating. Moreover, the exit conditions had to be reconsidered in terms of the number of directions for exiting and consequently the number of stairways needed. In order to provide legal means of exit from the auditorium, the front stairs had to be supplemented with an additional stairway going in the opposite direction. This meant that a space of suitable dimensions had to be found within the building, or a new space large enough to contain the stair had to be added.

After careful consideration and lengthy study, a decision was made to work the stair into the base of

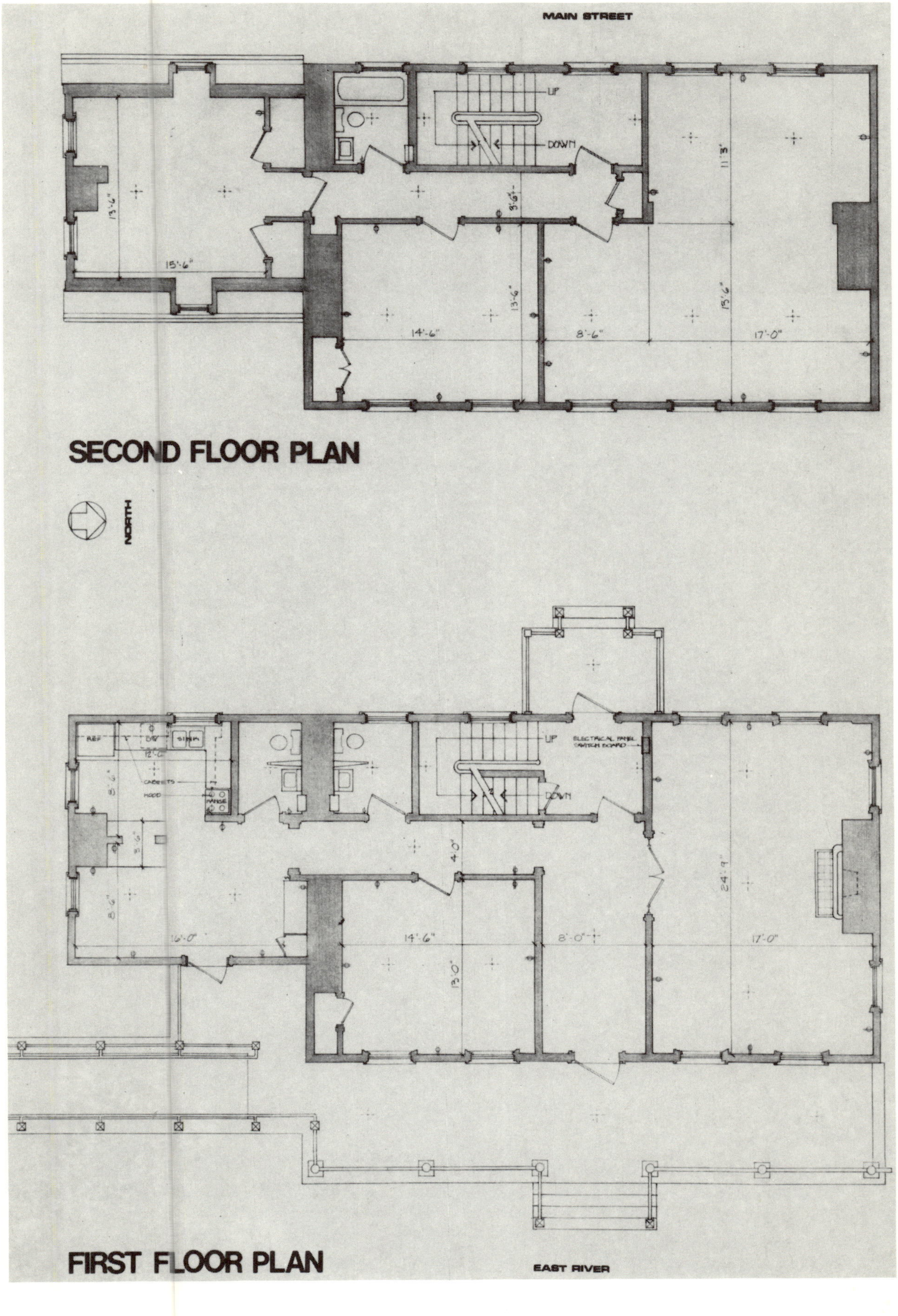
MAIN STREET
UP
DOWN
13'-6"
15'-6"
3'-6"
11'-3"
14'-6"
13'-6"
8'-6"
15'-6"
17'-0"
SECOND FLOOR PLAN
NORTH
UP
DOWN
16'-0"
4'-0"
14'-6"
13'-0"
8'-0"
24'-9"
17'-0"
FIRST FLOOR PLAN
EAST RIVER

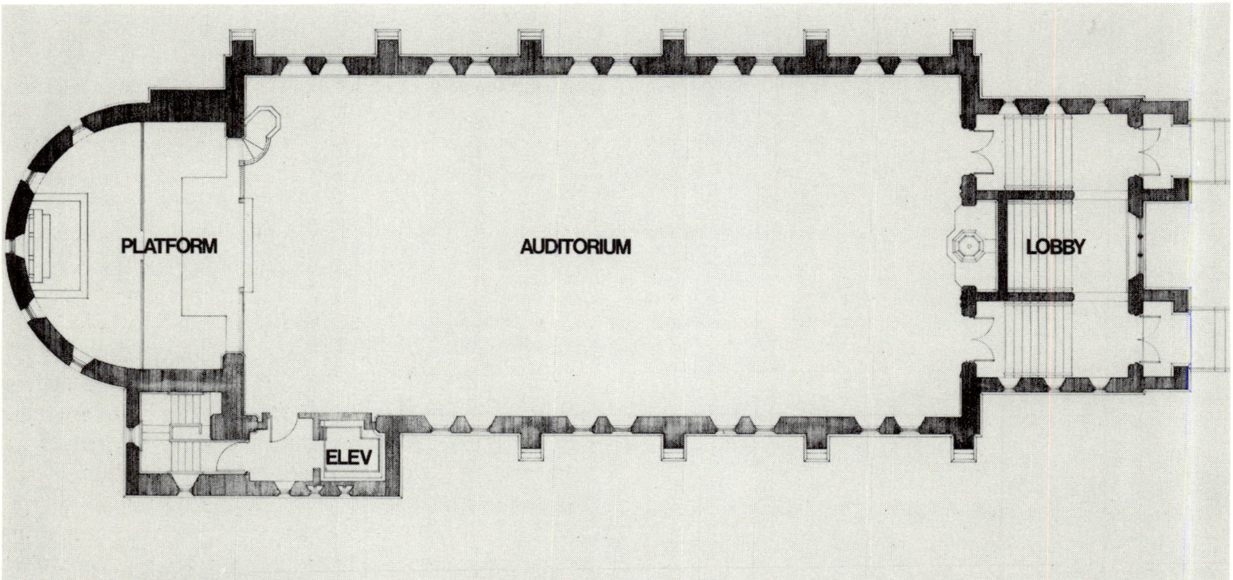

GROUND FLOOR PLAN

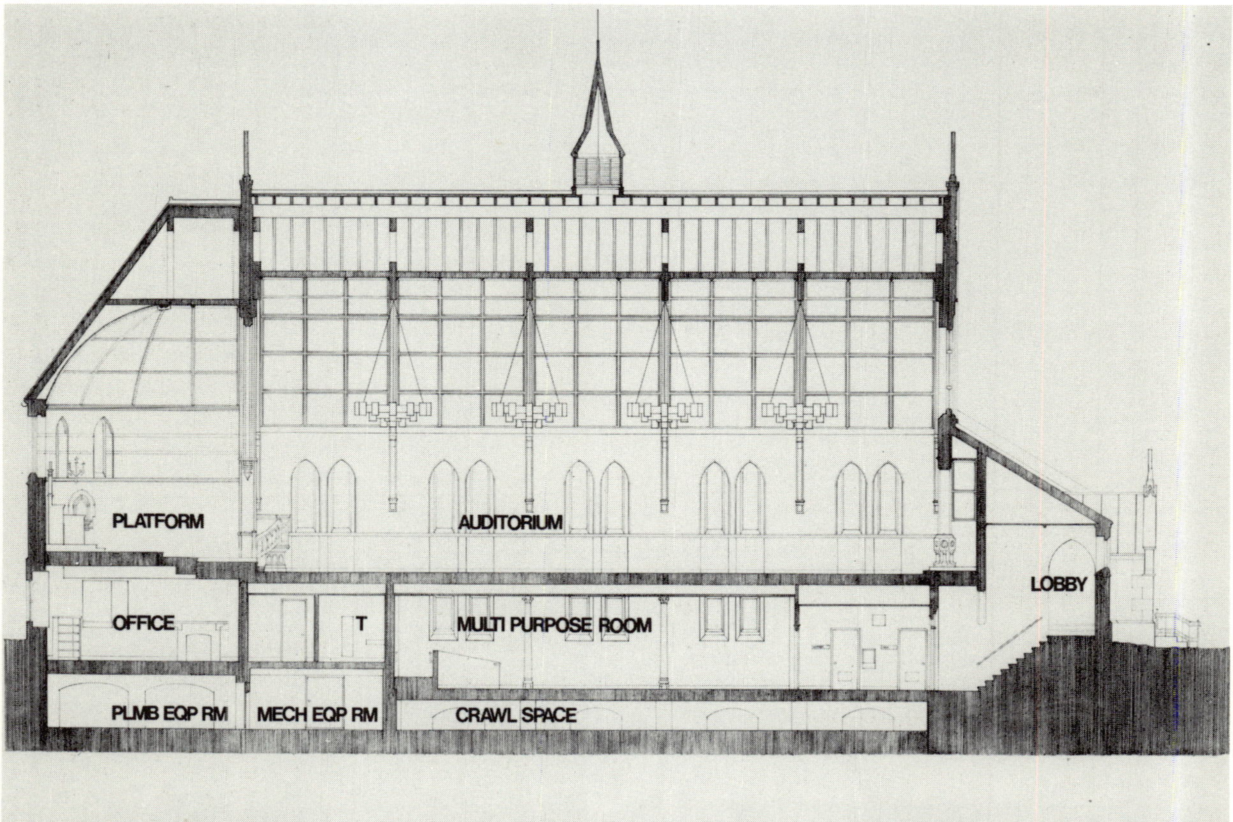

LONGITUDINAL SECTION

the bell tower in which were located service closets and a winding wooden stair connecting the apse to the lower floor. This demanded delicate structural work because the thick brick bearing walls had to be removed to obtain the minimum legal dimensions of the stair. The upper area of the tower was used to house the mechanical equipment necessary for ventilation and/or air-conditioning. The Middle Ages concept of the open shaft bell tower as a sound chamber for the bells had to be abandoned.

It must be understood that the solutions found to satisfy the state building code were related to the selected use for the building. If the auditorium had to be flexible enough to permit dramatic presentations on a commercial basis, a fourth exit probably would be needed and a new bulky addition to the existing building could not have been avoided. Whether this new shaft were designed in contemporary terms or in imitative ones, modification of the original concept of the architect would have been necessary.

Chapel of the Good Shepherd *(1875), Roosevelt Island, New York City. Restored for use as community center. First floor plan (left, above); longitudinal section (left, below). (Cavaglieri)*

Jefferson Market Courthouse

The transformation of the old Jefferson Market Courthouse into a regional branch of the New York City Public Library is considered one of the most satisfactory examples of adaptive reuse in New York. The profile of the old Greenwich Village clock tower has been seen in the photographs of many architectural magazines and newspapers throughout the country. It may be a shock to learn that when the plans for reconstruction were first filed at the Department of Buildings under the old New York City code, the examiner requested that the tower, as well as the attic inside the great trusses behind the sculptured gable, be cut down and a flat new roof installed to conform with the regulation that limited the height of a building used by the public to 40 feet when that structure contained wood floor-bearing members. Fortunately, this same building code gave discretionary powers to the Building Department chief engineer for the purpose of consulting with the architect of record about alterations to existing buildings and their structural safety. The engineer then in charge, the late Al Sills, took it upon himself to study the problems with the architect of the restoration and to consider the addition of such safety provisions as added exits and selectively located sprinkler heads. If the building were to have been used by the public for something other than a library, sprinklers would have been the most desirable fire protection device. But, according to some of the experts on that job, a library could not use sprinklers because of the risk of irreparable damage by water to books and other documents.

The discretionary power of the chief engineer was lost when the new New York City code was adopted in the early 1960s. This restriction is a damaging one for the landmark buildings of New York. Now the only recourse available to an architect involved in an adaptive reuse project is an appeal to the Board of Standards and Appeals, a process that requires the preparation of many documents and several months of bureaucratic action. The complexity of the procedure and the uncertainty of the results discourage private owners.

New York Shakespeare Festival

The New York Shakespeare Festival Public Theater accepted an invitation from the New York City Landmarks Preservation Commission to acquire the former Astor Library, which had been used as a hostel for immigrants for more than 40 years. Joseph Papp, the producer of the festival, was fascinated by the remainders of the multi-storied open-well spaces, offering the possibility of attractive auditoriums to the Public Theater. After the first schematic plans were developed and the envisioned layouts were related to

JEFFERSON MARKET COURTHOUSE *(1874), Greenwich Village, New York City. Restored for use as branch of New York City Public Library. (Gil Amiaga, architectural photographer, N.Y.C.) First floor plan and site plan (right, above); longitudinal section (right, below). (Cavaglieri)*

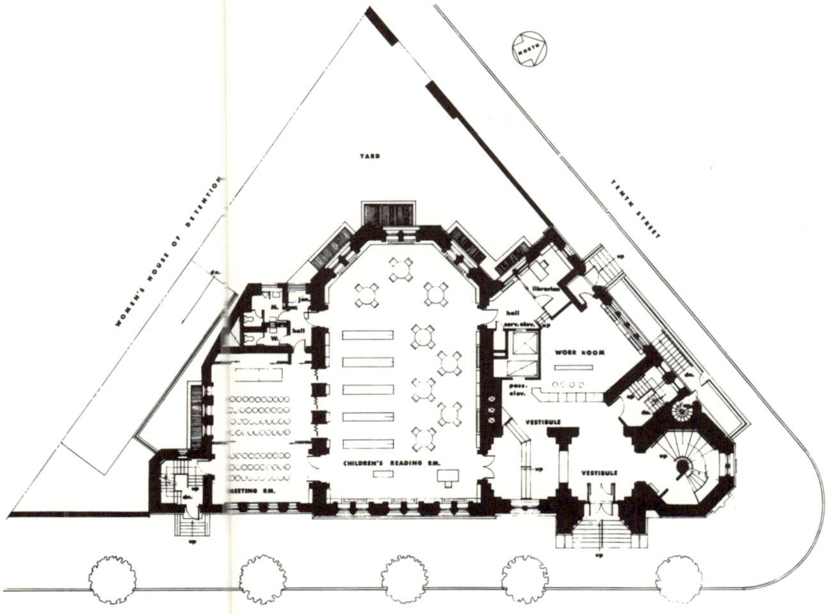

FIRST FLOOR PLAN & SITE PLAN

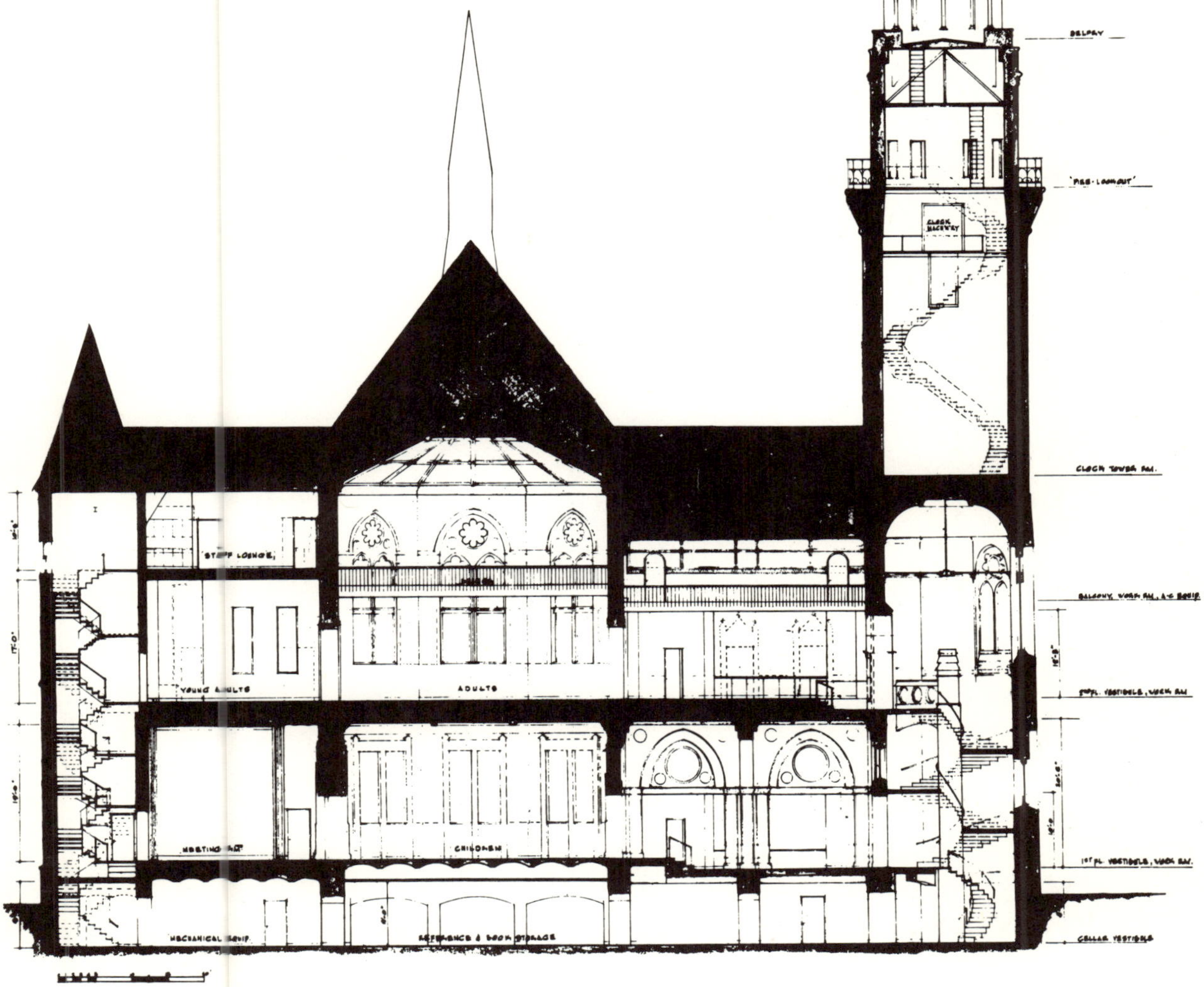

LONGITUDINAL SECTION

the building code regulations, it became evident that each of the three sections of this large structure enclosed an area larger than the maximum nonfireproof building permitted by the New York City code. Moreover, as each of the three floor levels of the building were approximately 20 feet high, it was also impossible to comply with the 40-foot height limitation specified by the code for a building with horizontal structural members made of combustible material.

The design, including the enclosure of stairs, the insertion of various doors and fire doors and the application of fire-retardant ceilings, was approved by the Building Department with the promise by the user to restrict occupancy (for example, rehearsal halls would be used by the same people who would act in the theatrical spaces at other times). After a while, Mr. Papp could not resist the temptation to stage dramatic performances in the rehearsal rooms, thus attracting extra patrons and collecting added applause. But the Fire Department, which has overriding powers in New York City and whose executive personnel do not analyze plans but only visit buildings, expressed dissatisfaction with the definition and use of the various spaces. The question had to be reopened and the problem reconsidered; new sprinklers had to be added and a new circulation was worked out at various levels of the building. These new instructions were received from the Board of Standards and Appeals after an application was filed and discussed with them, following complaints of the Fire Department.

New York Shakespeare Festival Public Theater, *Greenwich Village, New York City. Former Astor Library and hostel for immigrants restored for use as theater. (George Cserna)* **Longitudinal section** *(right, above); third floor plan (right, below). (Cavaglieri)*

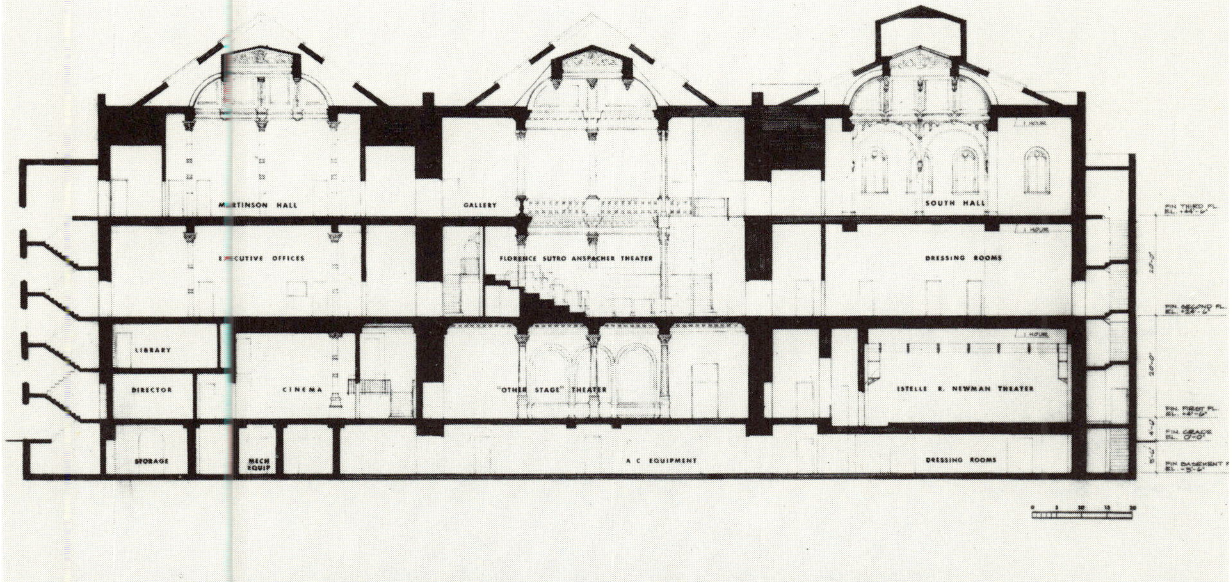

LONGITUDINAL SECTION

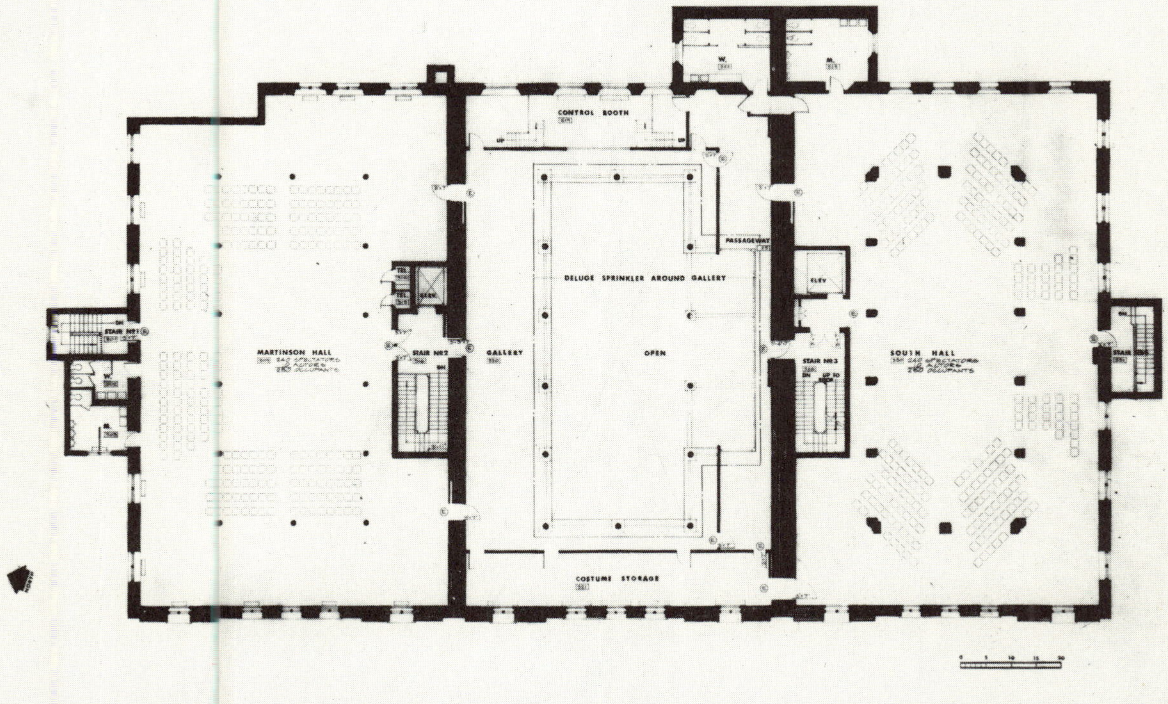

THIRD FLOOR PLAN

New York State Maritime Museum

Perhaps the largest project of preservation for adaptive reuse in which I have been engaged is the feasibility study for restoration of a city block in lower Manhattan as the New York State Maritime Museum. Filling approximately half of this block is the well-known Schermerhorn Row, a series of mercantile houses dating from 1812. The other half of the block with the exception of one empty corner is occupied by structures built for similar purposes in the middle and second half of the 19th century.

The projected new use would give more than a third of the available square footage at various levels to the Maritime Museum; the rest of the structures on the commercial area would be used for retail and

Schermerhorn Row *(1812), Manhattan, New York City. Block of mercantile houses restored for use as New York State Maritime Museum. (Amiaga) First floor plan (below). (Cavaglieri)*

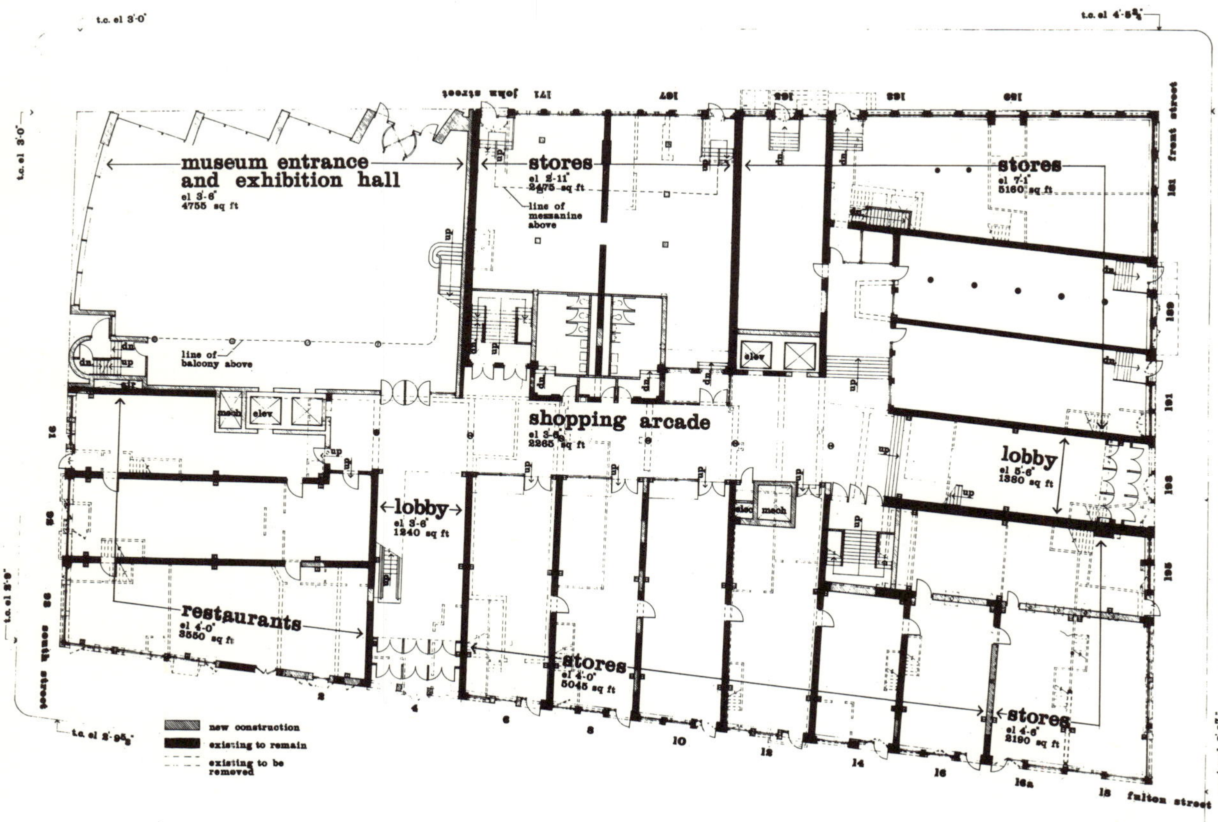

office tenancy. All the old buildings are nonfireproof. A renovation and reuse suitable to 20th-century economic needs will utilize the number of stairwells necessary for a single building that would fill the entire area. The necessity of providing occupants with safe exits in two directions, a common requirement of most current urban codes, precludes considering each of the original properties as an entity.

After long analysis and careful study, it was recommended that a noncombustible spine be built within the interior of the block to connect the new fireproof stairwells and to be accessible to the occupants of all the buildings.

The area to be used by the Maritime Museum includes the attic of the 1812 buildings and the vacant corner. The code requirements for live loading have necessitated the addition of structural elements such as columns, footings, etc. Naturally these elements will affect the appearance of the buildings and will alter many of the existing parts. If the use of the reconstructed building changes, so would the safety precautions and the required loading change.

Basic Code Requirements

In general terms, most building codes concentrate on the following basic subjects:

1. *Establishing categories of buildings according to occupancy.* This separates residential from public use and it determines, in accordance with purpose, the square footage to be allocated to each person occupying the building or its parts. The codes specify these conditions in tabular form. For an existing building, after the use is defined, one can calculate the legal number of occupants permitted for each space or level.
2. *Classification of construction.* The different parts of the building (walls, roof, floors, etc.) are classified by the number of hours, or fractions of hours, through which the specific materials will safely maintain their characteristics when exposed to fire. Again, definitions of fire resistance of various building elements are not related to a specific building in an absolute way, but are related to a building in different ways according to the uses planned for the spaces. At times, even the ownership or tenancy of spaces, single or multiple, affects the fire-resistance requirements; the care an owner-occupant can give a building is not considered comparable to the lack of care that can be expected from a tenant.
3. *Area heights and volume limitations.* These are related to the occupancy and construction classifications. They are based on the community's judgment of the density of existing or anticipated population and evaluation of the hazards that population creates.
4. *Exits.* Requirements for the number of exits, the placement in relation to the center of a space or floor, the size in relation to the number of occupants and the character of the exit corridors are based on the code writers' evaluation of the danger to human life in case of a fire emergency. As with volume limitations, each community and its representatives have arrived at compromises and judgments to establish the figures in the building code. All codes are similar in purpose, but they are far from identical. In almost all building codes, there are provisions that are based on different concepts and that therefore reach different conclusions.
5. *Provision for handicapped persons.* In recent years it has been recognized that the right of movement into and through a building, particularly a public one, should not be taken away from persons whose movements are hampered by physical disabilities. Many building codes demand design features in new buildings that permit use by the handicapped. When federal or public funds are desired for a building program, ramps and/or specially sized elevators and suitable sanitary facilities must be provided for use by wheelchair users.
6. *Live load.* All codes relate different live loads to the various uses of spaces through tabulations referring to floors, bearing walls, columns, etc. The design must be certified, stresses calculated and test certificates submitted.
7. *Sanitary facilities.* The number of fixtures must be related to the number of occupants using the facilities.
8. *Ventilation.* The natural or mechanical ventilation of all the spaces related to human occupancy is defined in codes by requirements concerning the size of fenestration, openable areas, size of ducts or shafts, changes of air, etc.

When an existing building executed before the codes were written is to be redesigned for reuse, all the items previously listed must be verified and/or corrected. The restoration architect must certify to compliance with the regulations, and the city official must be satisfied by such certification and testify to its accuracy in order to protect the user and the public. All these subjects have been considered by the code because they were judged by city officials to be important to the comfort and safety of the public.

Laypersons frequently suggest that preservation commissions or design boards should obtain special waivers from the various building departments so that original designs may be preserved. Any serious technical and artistic judgment, however, must recognize that even if the requirements of the code are oppressive or disturbing at times, the safety and comfort of the users cannot be disregarded. It therefore becomes the restoration architect's duty to make preservation compatible with code requirements and when selecting the design items of secondary importance to carefully choose those that can be changed in order to permit the required or desired protection. Only when this is done can preservation for adaptive reuse be considered successful.

Federal Preservation Projects and Building Codes: Independence Hall

LEE H. NELSON, AIA

Lee H. Nelson, AIA, is historical architect with the National Park Service and has been involved with the restoration of numerous historic buildings, including Independence Hall. He is presently technical editor of the forthcoming preservation handbook for federal agencies and state and local governments.

In the printed *Preservation & Building Codes* program, this presentation is titled "Federal Preservation Projects and Building Codes," but instead of giving a broad look at federal preservation, the paper will focus on the preservation and public use problems of one well-known federal historic building: Independence Hall.

Actually these problems are not very different from those of the small-scale or large-scale preservation projects that are described in others of these papers. Perhaps the public use is more intense at Independence Hall, but the other problems relating to preservation are somewhat the same. The main differences are the value judgments regarding the protection of the building and the public. However, this is not to suggest that there should be a double standard for such protection merely because some buildings (such as Independence Hall) are higher on a scale of historical significance.

Independence Hall is now under the complete custody of the U.S. Department of the Interior, National Park Service, although a fee-simple title is still retained by the City of Philadelphia. Since historic buildings in federal custody are exempt from local building codes, the Philadelphia Building Codes were not applicable and compliance was not required. However, these interests were partly represented by the city architect, who, as a member of the Architectural Committee of the larger Advisory Commission, reviewed proposals for the development of the park and its historic resources.

Policies

At the present time, guidance comes from *Administrative Policies for Historical Areas of the National Park System,* which were formulated and published in 1968. These policy statements are vitally important to the planning and development of historic resources, but it should be noted that these policies did not exist at the time preservation and restoration was begun on Independence Hall and the other historic buildings on Independence Square, which include Congress Hall and Old City Hall. At that time the Park Service was dependent on the professional judgments of its staff and an internal review system.

The first aspect of the policy that relates to "Building and Fire Codes" reads as follows: "In the preservation of historic structures, every attempt should be made to comply with local building and fire codes and to cooperate with local officials. However, compliance should not be allowed to destroy or impair the integrity of the structure. Where full compliance is not feasible, occupancy of the structure at any one time should be limited to the capacity of hall, stairways, and exits."

This paragraph is immediately followed by additional policy on "Fire Detection and Suppression," as follows:

> Where warranted by the significance or value of a historic structure or its contents, adequate fire warning and suppression systems should be installed. Where a manned fire station exists near the structure, a detection system providing a signal directly to the local fire authorities should be installed. Also, fire personnel should be advised of any peculiarities or dangers inherent in the structure and the features and contents whose value warrants the greatest care in the event of fire.
>
> Where local fire equipment and personnel are not readily available, the detection system should trigger a suppression system. A fog or freon system is preferable. Water sprinkler systems should be used only in structures whose fabric and contents are not likely to be irreparably damaged by water. Foam systems should be used only when the structure can be swiftly vacated.
>
> In planning and installing detection or suppression systems, the integrity of the structure and the requirements of its interpretation will be respected.

In addition, a separate section on "Health and Safety" states that it is the policy of the National Park Service to provide for the safety of the public it serves. However, there are potentially contradictory statements regarding safety versus the visual and structural integrity of a historic property: "In historic buildings and districts, safety equipment such as fire hydrants, extinguishers, standpipes, and detection systems must be concealed to prevent the visual impairment of the integrity of the structure or district. Visitor aids, such as handrails, paint strips, etc., will be avoided in historic structures unless they were part of the historic architecture or furnishings." These, then, are the current National Park Service policies for the protection of the resources and the public.

INDEPENDENCE HALL, *Philadelphia. Construction begun 1732, completed 1756. Part of Independence National Historical Park, located in downtown Philadelphia. (National Park Service, U.S. Department of Interior)*

History

Independence Hall can be presented as a case history, pointing out the structural problems, preservation needs and considerations for visitor use.

Independence Hall (originally called the Pennsylvania State House) was built in the 1730s and 40s; the tower and steeple were appended to the building in the 1750s. Actually the steeple was so deficient in either construction or maintenance that it was taken down in 1781 and the tower was capped with a spire and weathervane. The present familiar steeple dates from 1828 and was one of the earliest attempts at reconstruction specifically for historical purposes.

The building was variously used, abused and neglected; it received first a succession of renovations for adaptive use and then a succession of renovations for historical purposes, by the state, then by the city and finally by the National Park Service.

Construction

Independence Hall is a two-story masonry building with an attic, a cellar and the tower and steeple. Physically, it is similar to other large public and religious buildings of the period. The exterior walls are of brick masonry, well constructed and in good condition. The first floor originally consisted of two large rooms, a center hallway and a generous tower stairhall. The second floor had one full-length front room some 20 feet wide and 100 feet long (appropriately called the "Long Room"), two rear rooms and an entryway called the "Lobby."

On the first floor the cross-walls are of brick. When built, the second floor longitudinal partitions were structural, consisting of concealed wooden trusses. These trusses supported the first floor ceiling framing systems, which were also wooden and included heavy girders with an infilling of joists and secondary members. The second floor ceilings were also framed with wood, and the roof was supported with a system of wooden trusses. These structural systems suffered from years of neglect, changing occupancies and such overloading as the addition of an enormous flagpole supported by the roof trusses and the removal of the second floor wall trusses to provide larger courtrooms.

One might assume that such changes diminished the integrity of the fabric, yet a surprising amount of the original structure survived, including the masonry walls and foundations, the roof trusses, the second floor ceiling framing and the first floor ceiling framing. These survivors, however, have suffered from dry rot, cuts for plumbing and electrical installation, technical failures due to aging, overstressing, etc. In short, the building suffered in much the same way as many other historic structures.

Approach to Restoration

The preservation needs for Independence Hall were so extensive that an engineering survey in the 1950s recommended gutting and replacing all the structural systems with steel and concrete. This approach, of course, would have allowed compliance with some, if not all, aspects of the building and fire codes. Even without the benefit of the policy statements quoted previously, it was evident to a majority of technical and administrative personnel in the National Park Service that a historic building is a cultural artifact first and that preservation of the structural integrity cannot be easily separated from the symbolic and historical significance. Thus, it is first an artifact and second a container, in the sense of an enclosure built for human use.

Lacking a formulated policy, an ad hoc policy of maximum preservation of the historic fabric within the context of structural adequacy was followed. Actually, this resulted in some structural overdesign because other factors tend to reduce the maximum possible occupancy. This ad hoc preservation policy affected most design decisions with a relation to building codes, fire codes, health and safety codes. This seems to put the welfare of the building ahead of the welfare of the people who use it, and to a certain extent this is true. The problem is that people use a building, and use implies wear, and wear implies a diminishing of the resource. Even the process of restoration involves some destruction, some removal and some diminishing of the original fabric. The installation of a heating or air conditioning system

Major structural rehabilitation in 1962-63 halted deterioration and brought building up to structural and safety standards for visiting public. Goal was maximum preservation of original masonry walls and much of wood framing in second floor, attic and roof. (George Eisenman)

involves some cutting in the floors, walls or ceilings for ducts, wiring, grilles, etc.

Independence Hall has had at least six heating systems to supplement or replace the original fireplaces, and each one has subtracted from the historical integrity. Considering the state-of-the-art of mechanical systems, six more systems are easily foreseeable, each exacting its own toll. Therefore decisions were made to reinforce the original wooden structural systems, such as the floor and ceiling framing and roof trusses, and to preserve the wall finishes, the wooden stairs, the doors, the windows, the roofing, the steeple or any other part of the historic fabric. Missing parts were recreated using the same type of construction and the same kinds of finishes. Inevitably, there were numerous compromises due to gaps in knowledge, unavailability of materials, lost skills, mistakes or other factors beyond control; but most of the compromises were for the sake of strength, durability, ease of maintenance, considerations for visitor use, interpretation, safety and security. There was often a fine line between the ad hoc policy of preservation and practical or human values.

Thus, the rehabilitation involved a mixture of authenticity and practicality: wood, concrete and steel, wood carving, full electrical adequacy for television, low voltage for safe "period" lighting in some places, atmospheric control of temperature and humidity, wooden floors, heat and smoke detection. At no point was serious consideration given to the use of fire stairs, fire doors, fire escapes, reversal of door swings, panic hardware, etc. The Park Service did not believe then, nor does it believe now, that the public expects or wants a fire escape on Independence Hall, although such a device apparently was installed on a full-size replica of Independence Hall built in California a few years ago. Therefore, despite attempts to introduce safety and protective measures, there are still potential hazards (or inconveniences). There is more risk in visiting a historic property than there should be in visiting a modern replica, which has none of the inherent values of a cultural artifact.

Entryway Hazards

More than two million visitors a year cope with the main entrance latch and double doors. Opening the door requires depressing the thumb lever on the latch while grasping the handle and simultaneously pushing the door inward. This violates conditioned responses for entering or leaving buildings. Added to this entry problem, the door sill is higher than the entry platform and the interior floor level. While this was not uncommon for the period of construction, it is considered a hazard today. So a fiberglass ramp was installed to avert the possibility of injuries and tort claims. Perhaps the modern fiberglass ramp was not necessary, but the Park Service was not willing to compromise the historical level by raising the floor to match the sill, and some concession had to be made to public safety. Surely, this kind of empirical experience regarding safety should be recorded to guide future decisions. It should be noted that some of these decisions were influenced more by the quality of the historic environment than by the safety considerations.

Fire Protection

Areas that had no visitor access were supplied with fire suppression systems consisting of wet or dry sprinkler lines, depending on the location. In all visitor access areas, fire detection systems were installed, but no fire suppression systems. All detection systems, including those for the detection of certain mechanical equipment failures, humidity levels, etc., are continuously monitored at a central place. In areas of public access, fire suppression is manual, by either National Park Service personnel or the Fire Department of Philadelphia. Such interrelationships are close and must remain so even if detection technology becomes

Numerous visitors aggravate problems of internal circulation, open stairways, limited ingress and egress. (Lee H. Nelson, AIA)

Constantly observed master console monitors fire detection and suppression systems and atmospheric control systems for the park. (Nelson)

more sophisticated. In this case, the older technologies of fire suppression were central to the planning and development of this historic resource.

The preservation of the artifacts required complex systems of internal climate control, which in turn required substantial electrical energy service. These, too, have a snowball effect on the erosion of the historic fabric, visual intrusions and potential hazard of fire, explosion, vibration, failure, etc. Some of the more potentially dangerous aspects were ameliorated by building a new underground room for the centrifugal compressor and utilizing existing off-site underground rooms for the various banks of electrical transformers. All electrical circuits were distributed in copper-clad mineral-insulated cables with compression fittings, the merits of which have yet to be fully assessed in a historic and preservation context. Most new internal construction was a mixture of wood and steel with no special fireproofing, as all of the surviving original structure and finishes are combustible, including the furniture, woodwork and flooring. In some instances, particularly the new roof sheathing, it was feasible to use fire-rated treated wood, although the finish roofing was a mixture of copper for the upper roof slopes and wood shingles for the main roof slopes, which were completed before fire-rated wood shingles were available. Many of the external hazards have been reduced; for example, many neighboring buildings were removed, though not necessarily for this purpose; the fireplaces are inoperable; and fossil fuels are no longer used for heating. Thus, some high-risk materials (such as wood shingles) were used for the sake of authenticity, while other hazards were reduced.

Conclusion

Even though an administrative policy regarding building and fire codes in a preservation context did not exist and even though Independence Hall was technically exempt from the local code, the planning and design was as responsible and responsive to human safety as it was to the preservation of this irreplaceable historic resource. In the final analysis, both human and historic resources are irreplaceable.

One final comment: According to a newspaper account, Independence Hall came closest ever to destruction—by fire—in 1824. One night in that year, someone broke into the building, piled furniture in one of the open archways between the Central Hall and the Supreme Court Room and set fire to the furniture. An inebriated passerby saw the flames and gave the cry to awake the watchman, and thus notify the fire brigade. The fire was contained, causing only a slight charring of the archway. Thus the preservation of Independence Hall, with its present sophisticated gadgetry to assure its survival for future generations, would not be a topic for discussion today had it not been for the vigilance of an anonymous tippler 150 years ago.

Discussion

Comments made by the speakers and the audience during the discussion of current issues are here summarized.

When entering a historic building, one may ask, "What was it like 80 or 100 years ago?" Additions may often have been necessary to satisfy building codes, exit requirements and safety regulations, but the visitor should be able to tell which elements are original and which are of a later period. The Jefferson Market Library, designed by Withers and Vaux in 1874, is a mixture of Venetian-Gothic and German-Romanesque styles, but the bridge in the reading room of the library is a later addition, and there is nothing wrong with this being recognized.

In the reading room the bookshelves and the bridge are black in contrast to the rest of the room. The fluorescent fixtures, also black, were especially designed at the request of the library because the fluorescent bulbs are less expensive and heat less than incandescent bulbs, resulting in lowered operation costs for the building. A question that is often debated is: How does one interpret the modern elements that must exist? Unless the building presented to the public is used only as a museum, necessary additions must be interpreted in contemporary terms. Whether additions are successful or not always depends on the architect. The bridge in the reading room is an obvious contemporary element in that space. It is obviously 20th-century because spanning 40 feet with a 16-inch-deep structural member requires 20th-century technology. In some buildings for which codes require another staircase or another exit, it is more desirable to place it outside the building, hide it a little bit more or put it in the back. But each case is unique and must be analyzed differently.

Codes have developed in two ways: They are based on physical laws (such as how much weight a steel beam will carry) or they are empirically derived. The

JEFFERSON MARKET LIBRARY, *New York City. New elements of bookshelves, bridge and lighting fixtures are black, in contrast to architectural detail of reading room. (Marc Neuhof)*

official must observe the code and, excepting an official's disposition and willingness to take risks, that is the way the code is interpreted. Some official interpreters of the code are sympathetic to historic preservation; others are not. Sanitary examinations are no less strict than the structural ones.

In New York City a recent code revision abolished the requirement for approval of restoration projects by the code officials alone. Now code variances must be contested before the Board of Appeals, a process that may take as long as six months. Previously there was a possibility of straightening out a problem at the personal level. If an architect was confident of a position and able to substantiate it, the problem could be discussed and a quicker conclusion sometimes was possible. It is more difficult to appeal to a board that holds public hearings and, therefore, is subject to political pressures.

In some historic buildings, especially if they must accommodate large groups and certainly if they are constructed of flammable material, it would seem to be safer to let the door swing out even if it was originally fitted to swing in. One could put a sign next to it, stating, "Historically this door swung in, but for safety reasons it now swings out."

Sometimes, however, if the restoration of a federal building is not required to comply with codes and the authenticity of the building is an experience worth having, hazards can be minimized in other ways so as not to compromise historical fact. Such decisions depend on the building: the merits of each particular problem, the adaptive use and the egress and ingress problems. At the present time, historical authenticity is an extremely important part of National Park Service planning considerations. Unless a hazard is so overwhelming that it cannot be mitigated by trained personnel or by briefing before the public enters the building, the Park Service is reluctant to compromise the authenticity of a building. When a building is subject to code authorities it is unlikely that door swings are the only problem; characteristically, the mode of entry to the buildings has to be considered as well. Therefore, compliance with the code may also require revision of the portico. It is very difficult to define and limit such adjustments.

When there is a conflict between code regulation and occupancy classification, the National Park Service policy is to limit occupancy. The Park Service has both skilled personnel and tight control of access to its buildings. The problem is that many persons who have responsibility for a historic property open to the public feel compelled to funnel as many people through the building as possible. Overcrowding is a real safety problem, and limiting occupancy also increases the quality of the experience. For example, it is not particularly educational or inspiring to pass through Independence Hall like a herd of cattle. The Park Service is extremely conscious of the entry and exit problem and over a period of several years has studied reactions of visitors to the front door and to ramps inside and problems of the disabled, etc. Visitors cannot see whether a door should open in or out, especially if it has a big handle; they expect to pull the door. Sometimes a small instructional sign on the door is necessary. The problem can be solved by escorting visitors in a group; the guide opens the door and the problem is solved.

In some buildings the floor is lower than the threshold, a common practice in Europe but not as common here. Even though the higher threshold may be an original feature of the building, it can be dangerous and may require the addition of a fiberglass ramp—an obviously modern intrusion.

Current Solutions

VIEUX CARRÉ, *New Orleans. Street scene. (Vieux Carré Commission)*

An Architect's View of Preservation within Existing Codes

MURVAN M. MAXWELL, FAIA

Murvan (Morris) Maxwell, FAIA, is senior architect with Maxwell & LeBreton, Architects. He is a member of the Louisiana Historical Preservation and Cultural Commission, chairman of the Board of Building Standards & Appeals (Building Code Appeal Board) of New Orleans and vice chairman of the American Institute of Architects Codes and Standards Committee.

Many persons who are interested and concerned with the well being of historic resources are now directing more attention to the impact of modern safety and building regulations on the preservation effort. But, all too frequently an architect or a preservationist group develops a complete and detailed set of documents for the restoration and preservation of a historically important structure and then applies for a building permit without having conferred previously with the municipal building department. Upon being advised of numerous deviations from local code requirements, the architect expostulates that the structure is of precode vintage and thus exempt from current regulations and restrictions. The building official, taking the position that the law makes no exceptions for buildings in this category, applies the regulations without fear or favor. Thus, the often repeated conflict of authentic restoration versus adherence to modern building regulations.

Many building officials maintain that the architect or project sponsor all too frequently either fails or neglects to visit the building department before developing a complete set of documents to discuss the code problems usually attendant to a restoration or preservation effort. They contend that one or more preliminary conferences could resolve a number of the restrictions that would likely be imposed, thereby reducing the number of requirements that may have to be evaluated by a higher authority, especially in situations where legal provisions have been made for further review and possible relief by way of the appeals process.

Building officials like to be consulted about unusual or difficult situations prior to finalization of plans. They often become perturbed and even aggravated on learning that the fully completed package is being presented for consideration without any previous conferences. They often become less cooperative, ofttimes adamant and have a tendency toward strict application of code requirements.

Some building officials will not allow any variance whatsoever from a specific code requirement or regulation and even are reluctant to concur in an appeal to a higher authority. The situation becomes even more acute when such officials are not historic resources-minded. Preservationists have every right to view such an attitude with deep concern and to undertake a course of action that will result in an equitable solution.

The Board of Building Standards and Appeals of the city of New Orleans works with a building department that is sympathetic to the problems involved in historic preservation and authentic restoration. The chief plan examiner of the city encourages conferences during the early planning and development stage and gives advance notification of problem areas. Although he is open-minded and not dedicated to code enforcement down to the letter, this official's authority is limited, and involved or difficult situations are channeled to an appeals board. With the large quantity of restoration activity in New Orleans, the chief plan examiner frequently must refer questionable items to the appeals board.

The Vieux Carré is a historic district regulated by a legally constituted commission. Nevertheless, that commission cannot set aside safety and fire code regulations, nor can it override building code provisions. Additionally, New Orleans has the Garden District plus a number of noteworthy structures scattred throughout the city, and preservationists in New Orleans quickly rally when these historic places are threatened with destruction or when attempts are made to alter them beyond recognition. While not always successful, these preservationists go to the building department when they think codes and regulations are being too literally or too strictly enforced. Again, the appeals board is often involved.

We should remind ourselves to be practical about preservation. Should we preserve from the ravages of time, but lose to the ravages of fire that reduces the preservation effort to zero? If an original feature authentically restored by today's standards is a hazard and if litigation and cancellation of liability insurance coverage ensue as a direct result of that action, then we have not fulfilled our duty to the client and to the public. If an original winding stairway is to be retained, rendering it safe for public use is essential even though the original design must be somewhat compromised. An architect's professional liability is as great in historic building restoration as in any other commission, and certain basic safety measures must never be bypassed.

In addition, the members of an appeals board must be mindful of their obligation to the public when they decide how far to stretch the intent of modern building laws and standards to cover structures erected many decades prior to the promulgation of those requirements.

It can be difficult to convince an appeals board that to carefully and expertly conceal or blend an automatic sprinkler system, early-warning devices or emergency illumination is not as important a preservation measure as the exact restoration of a fireplace or dormer window. Occasionally, a change in use of a historic structure results in the original structural system's being inadequate for the new purpose. For example, if the existing floor framing will not support the proposed loading the appeals board will probably deny the proposed change unless the structural inadequacies are rectified. Saying that it ought to hold up, even though an appropriate safety factor is being exceeded, is not sufficient reason to abridge a safety consideration.

Fortunately, almost all preservationists recognize electrical hazards and so are hesitant to oppose safe electrical installations. Ample evidence attests that a modern and safe electrical system can be incorporated into a restoration project without clashing with its authenticity. An exception are the illuminated exiting and directional signs. It takes great skill to conceal, disguise or otherwise blend this type of safety device into a historic structure.

A detached or isolated structure presents a different situation from a structure that will expose its neighbor or expose nearby property (historic or otherwise) to a possible fire hazard. Regulations for the two situations naturally vary, but the former case is one in which restraints should be placed on overzealous enforcement officials. It is not uncommon to find a frame structure worthy of preservation located within a municipality's most restrictive fire zone and close to neighboring property. If an exposure hazard exists, an enforcement official can readily impose requirements that will impede a restoration project. In this case, a knowledgeable and sympathetic appeals board usually can initiate means to meet the intent of a code and establish guidelines for the protection of adjoining property without adverse effect on the proposed preservation effort.

Some enforcement departments take issue with a minor variation in stair riser and tread height, an insufficient number of plumbing fixtures, a substandard ceiling height or an excess in height and area based on the existing type of construction. The Department of Safety and Permits of the city of New Orleans concentrates on variations or code departures of major significance. Considering the large volume of preservation and restoration work in the city, major departures from code requirements occur frequently and thus the appeals board frequently must resolve an unusual or critical situation. The board arrives at a workable solution much more often than it denies an appellant's request for a variation and it has a good working relationship with the state fire marshal.

Persons interested in historic preservation and restoration are aware of the fact that many insurance companies consider historic structures a bad risk if code requirements have not been met. Frequently, it is difficult to obtain fire, extended coverage and builder's risk insurance. Additionally, some insurance companies place a limit on the amount of coverage available. Other insurance companies have maps in their offices with an "X" on Vieux Carré meaning "no policies written in this area." Others say, "Yes, we will take the risk, but maybe you would like to insure it for X-dollars." When the response is, "No, we can only cover it to Y-dollars," the owner is self-insured for the remainder. Obviously, such action dampens the activities of a local group that may want to maintain what it deems to be a meritorious structure.

In most states, the state fire marshal follows the Safety to Life Code as promulgated by the National Fire Protection Association (NFPA), frequently referenced as NFPA-101. On the other hand, cities and towns usually adopt building codes based wholly or in part on one of the four model codes. In many respects the NFPA standard and the local codes are not compatible. It is not unusual for a jurisdiction enforcing a building code with relaxed provisions for an old law or historic structure to find requirements conflicting with the state fire marshal.

Only a few states have adopted or promulgated statewide building codes. So for the many historic structures in sparsely settled areas, the state fire marshal has jurisdiction. Whether a preservation or restoration project will be subjected to strict enforcement of regulations depends largely on the attitude of the state fire marshal. While a few state fire marshals have advisory boards, the appeal system is usually nonexistent at the state level.

For this reason, I have been conducting, through the Codes and Standards Committee of the American Institute of Architects, a campaign for AIA participation in the NFPA Committee on Libraries, Museums and Historic Buildings. In addition to being a member of the NFPA Safety to Life Committee, I am also a member of its sectional committee on means of egress. Because regulations involving means of egress have a direct and decided impact on historic building preservation, I am urging liaison between the NFPA means of egress unit and the NFPA historic buildings group. I think the AIA representative on the NFPA Historic Buildings Committee should serve as an alternate member of the Means of Egress Committee and thereby keep posted on matters affecting historic preservation. The latest word from the AIA Historic Resources Committee and the AIA Codes and Standards Center is that NFPA representation is being advocated.

In the continued interest of historic preservation, the National Trust for Historic Preservation should become an active member of the National Fire Protection Association. It is eligible for membership.

New Orleans Historic Preservation and the Building Code

W. I. KELLEY

W. I. Kelley is coordinator and technical assistant to the New Orleans Board of Building Standards and Appeals. He was formerly chief of the Plan Processing Section for New Orleans, La.

The New Orleans municipal preservation law, enacted in 1937 for the area known as the Vieux Carré, was the first legislation in the United States creating a commission to protect "buildings having architectural and historic worth." The duty of a building official is the enforcement of that legislation in application of the New Orleans Building Code. This duty implies a quandary: enforcing a building code that regulates safety, versus enforcing an ordinance for preservation. Methods to make safe, yet retain, must be found. Similarly, as a result of new municipal legislation ending demolition in the central business district, the building official must cooperate with interested professionals in keeping many 19th-century buildings in use, yet enforcing legally applicable safety standards.

The New Orleans Building Code is based essentially on the 1940 Uniform Building Code, which states that "Buildings in existance [sic] at the time of passage of this code may have their existing use of occupancy continued, if such use or occupancy was legal at the time of passage of this code, provided such continued use is not dangerous to life." This statement is repeated verbatim in the 1973 Uniform Building Code. Herein lies any latitude for enforcement that a building official may have. It cannot be imagined that any historic building in New Orleans would not precate the modern safety ordinance, which originated in 1910. Consequently, all historic buildings qualify for the exception rather than the rule, unless major occupancy changes are proposed. Thus, the building official is not approached unless conversion, alterations or additions are proposed, and a building permit is necessary.

In New Orleans, conditions involving no changes are investigated and sanctioned at the inspection level by a committee of city and state safety personnel, working jointly. Occasionally, if a doubt concerning safety arises, the building official or the Board of Building Standards and Appeals must be consulted.

Compromise is always possible, but does not lend itself to structural safety. For example, if the Vieux Carré Commission, the legal watchdog for the Vieux Carré, has ordered a facade to be retained, embodied in a new building, methods must be found to retain it safely. The building official should meet with design professionals to find a mutually satisfying method of retention, with safety in mind and the attitude that such a method can and must be found.

In the recent past, requests for a number of renovations in the Vieux Carré reflected a change of building use to higher density, residential occupancy. These multistory buildings were so small that enforcing the exit requirements of the code would have resulted in abandonment of the project entirely. A committee of architects, working with city and state officials, developed a local standard to alleviate the conflict. All authorized agencies sanctioned this standard in jointly preparing the draft. It appeared unreasonable and unrealistic to order alterations to meet code exit standards. A standard was evolved employing principles of containment coupled with a partial sprinkler system, rendering reasonable means of exit and safety while keeping the structure in use.

None of the four model codes, i.e., National Building Code, Uniform Building Code, Southern Standard Building Code and BOCA Basic Building Code, have specific guidelines for safety in historic buildings. Some relief of modern code requirements can be gained through the Building Exits Code, 1959 edition, which does, to a degree, indicate adequacy of existing exits for substandard conditions. Principles of this nature can be employed whenever possible.

The necessity of conferences between building officials and design professionals in proposed conversions and alterations cannot be too strongly emphasized. Minor changes and rearrangements in the design stage result in a closer agreement with building code guidelines. Often, project architects for renovations are unaware of the latitude that may be exercised by a building official in application of the building code. This professional may also be unaware of behind-the-scenes actions, the constant interchange in ideas, rationalizations and interpretations between building officials and the Board of Building Standards and Appeals, the official interpreter of the code in New Orleans. Again, the professional may be unaware of the possibility of conferences with other city and state agencies having jurisdiction over safety, to arrive at mutual solutions. These contacts or conferences are of extreme importance, frequently resulting in savings and avoidance of disappointment to all interested parties.

There will always be cases that cannot be made to fit the framework of the codes and guidelines that the building official employs. These cases must, of course, be referred to the appeals board, for New Orleans the Board of Building Standards and Appeals. This happens, generally, when buildings are exceedingly large or the proposed change in use is severe. Today, with many advanced tools of fire protection,

orleans
gallery
inc

MERIEULT HOUSE *(1792), Vieux Carré, New Orleans. One of four structures surviving 1794 fire; restored to house Historic New Orleans Collection (left). (The Historic New Orleans Collection) View of Vieux Carré historic district (above). (Vieux Carré Commission)*

fire detection and early warning devices, the board can legally sanction their implementation as safety provisions, when the building official cannot.

For example, the historic Rabassa residence is being relocated in conjunction with the new Louis Armstrong Park. Fortunately, the site of the proposed relocation is about 300 feet north of the line designating the Inner Fire Limits, or most restrictive fire zone. If proposed relocation had fallen within that designated area, the building official would have been forced to deny the permit unless favorable consideration were given by the Board of Building Standards and Appeals. Another instance is Preservation Hall, a museum-assembly building being renovated in conjunction with the same project. A change in occupancy classification, under the building code, was not involved. This two-story, masonry building is required to be one-hour first-resistance protected throughout. The beaded wood, which was to be cleaned and reinstalled, was permitted provided it was installed over one-hour fire-rated gypsum board. A bad skew stair was allowed to remain, improved by an additional rail, installed to prohibit travel within 12 inches of the narrow end of the winders. These efforts are minor examples of working together for the general good.

New Orleans is fortunate in having its background of early fire protection legislation. Such legislation dates from 1789 in regulating roof coverings. Also, at some unknown date legislation was enacted requiring and acknowledging the value of masonry wall construction. It so happens that prime historical areas in New Orleans are generally within the city's most restrictive fire zone. All too often, preservationists lose sight of or are unaware of the special code requirements of the Vieux Carré. It is logical to assume that many Vieux Carré buildings would not exist if it were not for previously enacted safety standards, primarily preventing destruction by fire.

The areas of compromise are permitted by the statement in the building code recognizing existing buildings. If there is to be replacement, in total or in part, the building code is explicit in its requirements. It is only when "existing" is interpreted as "allowed to remain" that latitude can be exercised. In this city, the policy has been established that some leeway can be permitted as long as there is improved safety that approaches compliance with the building code.

A building official must perform in an atmosphere of conflict: charged by legislation and conscience to preserve that which is irreplaceable and also charged by legislation, knowledge and experience to enforce all safety standards. Fortunately, these conditions do not exclude each other and in themselves provide both a protection of life and a protection of property, specifically when a structure regarded as irreplaceable has been preserved and safety requirements have been upgraded.

A building official must travel in the fine area of not being so lax in enforcement as to disregard safety nor so strenuous that alterations and general upgrading of historic buildings are discouraged. A building official's responsibility to the community is, insofar as possible, to prevent abandonment of renovation, blight of unoccupied, deteriorating structures and demolition by neglect.

Pioneer Square Historic District, *Seattle, Wash. View of center of district. (Carleton Knight, III—National Trust)*

Preservation Legislation for Pioneer Square Historic District in Seattle

ARTHUR M. SKOLNIK

Arthur M. Skolnik is district manager of the Pioneer Square Historic District in Seattle, Wash. A licensed architect, he has been a participant in many national and international conferences and seminars on historic preservation and urban conservation.

EDMUND J. WOOD

Edmund J. Wood, attorney, is administrative assistant to Mayor Wes Uhlman of Seattle, Wash. He was formerly special counsel to the mayor for the Seattle Model City Program.

On the first day of May in 1970, Mayor Wes Uhlman signed Ordinance 98852 creating the Pioneer Square Historic District. Twenty blocks at the southern end of the Seattle central business district were thus declared to be of such importance that any "alteration, demolition, construction, reconstruction, restoration, remodeling or modification of structures [was prohibited] without a Certificate of Approval. . . ."

Ordinance 98852 states that even though Seattle is a relatively young city and "has had little time in which to develop many areas of consistent historical or architectural character," the district around Pioneer Square does contain structures of historical and architectural significance and should be safeguarded. As stated in section 1, the Pioneer Square Historic District was established "in order that the Pioneer Square area and buildings . . . may not be injuriously affected; to promote the public welfare, and to provide for the enhancement of this area and its structures, thereby contributing to the social, cultural and economic welfare of the citizens of Seattle."

The City Planning Commission was designated as the agency responsible for making recommendations regarding exterior alterations to the city council, after working in concert with the Historic Preservation Board. The board was to be composed of five members appointed by the mayor and to have review power over "all architectural and historic preservation matters within the Historic District."

The designation of the Pioneer Square area as a historic district was based on criteria established by the National Register of Historic Places. To quote section 4, "Districts, sites, buildings, structures, and objects of national, state and local importance are of historical significance if they possess integrity of location, design, setting, materials, workmanship, feeling and association" and fulfill one of four other criteria that concern artistic merit, educational value and historical association.

Section 5 describes the way each requirement was satisfied when the criteria were applied to the Pioneer Square area:

a. The Historic District has played a significant role in the development of Seattle, the Puget Sound Region and the State of Washington as the place of the beginning of Seattle; the place of the first industry, business and homes; the focus of commerce and transportation for more than half a century; the area that was rebuilt after the fire of 1889.

b. The Historic District is associated with the lives of many of the Seattle pioneers through property, business and commercial activities that were concentrated in that area.

c. Most of the buildings within the Historic District embody the distinctive characteristics of the late Victorian style and many are the work of one architect, Elmer H. Fisher. For these and other reasons, the buildings combine to create an outstanding example of an area in Seattle which is significant and distinguishable in style, form, character, and construction, representative of its era. The Historic District does possess integrity of location, original construction, and a feeling of association.

d. The restoration and preservation of the Historic District will yield information of educational significance regarding the way of life and the architecture of the late Nineteenth Century as well as adding interest and color to the city. Restoration of the Historic District will preserve the environment which was characteristic of an important era of Seattle's history and will be considerably more meaningful and significant educationally than if done for individual buildings.

As first written, the ordinance allowed new construction or alteration of buildings to proceed only on issuance of a Certificate of Approval "authorized by the Council following recommendations by the Commission." The ordinance was amended in April 1971 to designate the director of community development as the responsible party rather than the city council, and the approval of changes became a duty of that office.

As amended, section 6 of the ordinance requires that "all applications for building or demolition permits involving structures or sites within the Historic District shall be forwarded immediately by the Superintendent of Buildings to the [Historic Preservation] Board. " If the planned alterations are to be "minor work," a notice of intent is still required, but the request is reviewed by the Historic Preservation Board rather than the City Planning Commission. Minor work is defined by the ordinance as being "any work resulting in a modification of the exterior appearance of a building, including painting, where such work may lawfully be done without a building or demolition permit." Those alterations to be considered by the commission are evaluated according to:

> . . . the purposes of [the] ordinance and shall consider among other things the historical and architectural value and significance, architectural style, the general design, arrangement, texture, material and color of the buildings or structure in question or its appurtenant fixtures, including signs, the relationship of such features to similar features of other buildings within the Historic District, and the position of such building or structure in relation to the street or public way and to other buildings and structures.

When a proposed change is found by the commission not to be consistent with the stated purpose of the historic district, "the Director shall request the Commission or Board to consult with the owner within a period of 60 days for the purpose of considering means of preservation that will be in keeping with the Criteria." If, within that time or the available extension period, an acceptable solution has not been found, the Certificate of Approval will be denied. The recourse available to the property owner is an appeal of the decision to the full city council, whose determination to reverse or modify the first decision is made only if two conditions are met:

1. every reasonable effort has been made by the applicant to agree to the recommendations of the director, and
2. owing to special conditions pertaining to his piece of property, the full application of the recommended requirements will cause undue and unnecessary hardship.

Reinterpretation of Seismic Requirements

On July 5, 1973, Ordinance 102219, "relating to additions, alterations, repairs and maintenance of existing buildings, prescribing less restrictive seismic design requirements therefore and amending Sections 104 and 203 of the Building Code" became effective in the city of Seattle. The intent of the ordinance was to encourage the restoration of older structures through a reinterpretation of the seismic requirements. Section 104, which deals with the treatment of existing buildings, states, "Buildings or structures to which additions, alterations or repairs are made shall comply with all the requirements for new buildings or structures except as specifically provided in this section. . . ."

In section 1 the ordinance details those situations in which the building code is less stringently administered, although still in effect:

> (a) Additions, alterations, and repairs of an estimated cost not exceeding 50 percent of the true and fair market value of an existing building or structure. . .
> (b) Non-structural alterations and repairs: 25 percent or less of the true and fair market value of an existing building or structure . . . and
> (c) Minor structural additions, alterations and repairs. . .

Section (d) outlines the amended earthquake resistive requirements, stating "Where additions, alterations or repairs are made to buildings constructed prior to July 26, 1967, such buildings need only comply with earthquake resistive requirements as specified in Section 2312 (d) 2."

Special Review Districts

The third major piece of legislation passed to promote the preservation of Pioneer Square was approved by the city council August 21, 1973. Ordinance 102455 authorized the creation of special review districts and established the Pioneer Square Special Review District:

> To conserve and enhance the appearance of the City of Seattle, which is unique by virtue of its natural marine and mountain setting and its topographic features; to preserve areas of historical note or architectural merit; to protect and enhance neighborhoods, major public centers, parks, boulevards, waterfront areas; to encourage beneficial economic development; to assist property owners and tenants in maintaining the character of commercial, industrial, manufacturing, warehousing and residential areas; to promote the stability of land values and investments; to assist in the redevelopment of declining areas of the City where traditional zoning frequently is inadequate to accomplish such objectives; to promote the general welfare by safe guarding such areas for the future use and enjoyment of all our people; and to encourage community spirit, cooperation and participation, the Council may from time to time, as warranted, establish special review districts by ordinance to provide an additional measure of land use and development incentives and control in such districts.

The development guidelines in section 24.83 are established either by the city council or by the special review district board after at least one public hearing:

> [The guidelines] shall identify the unique values of the district, shall include a statement of purpose and intent, and shall be consistent with the purposes of the special review district. The guidelines may identify uses, structures and design characteristics which either have a positive or negative effect upon said values and may specifically modify bulk and use regulations and other provisions of the zoning ordinance in order to allow and encourage or to limit or exclude such structures, designs and uses.

GRAND CENTRAL ARCADE, *Pioneer Square, Seattle, Wash. (Carleton Knight, III — National Trust)*

Section 24.91 deals specifically with the creation of a special review district in the Pioneer Square Historic District. This additional means of legislative control was adopted primarily

> To ameliorate the adverse impact which the construction of the King County domed stadium is expected to have upon the cultural and ethnic values of the Pioneer Square area and the economic well-being of the industrial area south of the Pioneer Square Historic District, and to avoid proliferation of vehicular parking and other automobile-oriented uses at the expense of viable pedestrian uses and structures, displacing people; to encourage a variety of housing types related to all income groups; to encourage the use of transportation modes other than the private automobile; to exercise a reasonable degree of control over site development and the location of off-street parking and other automobile-oriented uses in said area and to achieve the purposes stated in the [General Purposes of Special Review Districts], there is hereby established the Pioneer Square Special Review District. . . .

Four specific development guidelines were written directly into the ordinance, ranging from those concerning the location of automobile-oriented facilities to the compliance requirements for nonaccessory parking lots to the regulation of street-level parking garages.

Minimum Maintenance Amendment for Pioneer Square

The most recent amendment related to preservation to be approved by the city council became effective on February 4, 1974. Ordinance 102902 amended three sections of an earlier ordinance and added three new sections. The amendment "establishes minimum standards for preservation and maintenance of buildings and structures in Pioneer Square Historic District and established enforcement procedures."

The amendment was a positive step to forestall any increased decay within the historic district. Section 6B provides that where certain conditions threaten the preservation of a building and the safety of its occupants, the occupants of adjacent buildings or the public, the structure is to be declared a "substandard historic district building." The determination of structural deficiencies is a responsibility of the superintendent of buildings, who after investigation may declare a historic building to be substandard. Notice is then given to the owner of record, stating the ways in which the structure is substandard and "setting forth the repairs, alterations or improvements . . . required to correct such substandard conditions or preserve the building and a reasonable period of time within which such required work shall be done."

View from pergola in Pioneer Square. (National Trust Archives)

A time and place for a public hearing is then set, with further action by the superintendent prohibited until after a decision by the Historic Preservation Board. It is the board's role to determine whether the action instituted by the superintendent was justifiable and whether the required remedial steps were reasonable. If the ruling upholds the decision of the superintendent and the owner refuses to comply, the procedure outlined in section 6C, "Historic District Maintenance and Repair Revolving Fund," is used to rectify the situation.

If the city is forced to spend funds for the repair, alteration or improvement of any substandard historic district building, the moneys are to be allocated from the Pioneer Square Historic District Revolving Fund, and the fund is to be reimbursed with:

1. Such sums as may be recovered by the City as reimbursement for costs and expenses of repair, alteration or improvement of Historic District buildings and structures found to be substandard;
2. Such other sums as may by ordinance be appropriated to or designated as revenue of such fund; and
3. Such other sums as may by gift, bequest or grant be deposited in such fund. . . .

Prior to April 1973, the Washington state laws provided that when a city incurred costs for repairs, alterations, improvements, vacating, closing, removal or demolition the charge would be assessed against the value of the real property involved. The assessment would be entered on the tax rolls against the property for the current year, becoming a part of the general taxes, with interest not to exceed 6 percent and with the owner having the prerogative to request that payment be divided into 10 equal annual installments. Washington State Senate Bill No. 2452 amended this procedure to increase the rate from 6 to 10 percent, requiring payment to be made in full.

One ramification of the minimum maintenance amendment has been that the demolition of buildings has become a more expensive procedure, causing owners to search more diligently for ways to preserve their structures.

Expansion of Historic District Boundaries

In May 1973 the City of Seattle Department of Community Development presented "Proposed Expansion: Pioneer Square Historic District—Report and Recommendations." The department had initiated the expansion study a year earlier, and it was conducted in the same manner as the original 1969 investigation. Buildings were identified and analyzed in terms of their historical and architectural integrity, resulting in an updated review and documentation of almost 200 structures.

The report proposed to expand the boundaries primarily for two reasons:

(1) to further integrate and strengthen the historic district through the addition of those architectural

> and historic structures and open spaces which were immediately adjacent to the area, but not protected by its legislation; and
> (2) to lessen the anticipated impact of the King County Domed Stadium through the creation of a buffer zone.

Subsequent to the presentation of the original expansion proposal, various other boundaries were proposed by the Department of Community Development. A subsequent vote by the city council, which makes the final decision, eventually decreased those boundaries.

Proposed Amendments to Original Ordinance

The most recent proposed legislation involves amending Ordinance 98852, for after nearly four years of operation a few administrative and definitional points needed to be clarified. The February 1974 draft proposes to:

> increase the membership and establish terms for the Pioneer Square Historic Preservation Board, . . . provide for reappointment and reconfirmation of existing members, . . . regulate the erection, placement or changing of signs in said District, and . . . provide civil penalties in place of criminal penalties for violations.

As originally written, Ordinance 98852 specified the appointment of one architect and two citizens at large. The proposed amendment will enlarge the Historic Preservation Board by increasing the participation of each category by one. This step seems desirable as the decisions requiring Board action become more complex and far-reaching with continued expansion and diversification of the historic district. Coupled with this increased board membership is a provision for designated terms of office and a mechanism for reconfirmation and reappointment of board members.

The second aspect of the proposed amendment is an attempt to further clarify and strengthen the Historic Preservation Board power to approve changes to buildings, structures and other visible elements within the historic district. As originally written, the ordinance requires the board to maintain control over "any material change in the exterior appearance of any existing structure" and the construction of new structures. As amended, the ordinance would also apply to "any visible change" and the erection and placement of any sign or change of message on any existing sign. The definition of a sign would also be clarified by section 6 of the proposed amendment:

> . . . a "sign" is any medium, including its structure and component parts, which is used or intended to be used to attract attention to the subject matter for advertising, identification or informative purposes, consisting of words, letters, figures, designs, symbols, notions, illuminations or projected images and including but not limited to banners, pennants, balloons, streamers and strings of light bulbs. . . .

The provisions of this ordinance are intended to apply to any sign which is located out of doors, or if indoors, within three feet of a window and visible from a street, sidewalk or other public place.

Preservation with the Virginia Statewide Building Code: The Architect's View

MILTON L. GRIGG, FAIA

Milton L. Grigg, FAIA, is senior architect with Grigg, Wood & Browne. He is chairman of the Building Code Review Board, Charlottesville, Va.

The Virginia building code has created persuasive precedents that may be adapted in other jurisdictions. It is the purpose of this paper to share experiences in conducting preservation and reconstruction projects under the new code.

The History

For several years the Virginia General Assembly sought to enact a statewide building code to relieve the chaos of municipalities and jurisdictions operating under not only one or more of the standard codes, but in many cases under locally conceived codes. Codes frequently reflected the prejudices either of political interest or of conservative building officials. State fire safety regulations administered by the State Corporation Commission further confused the situation. Efforts for legislation were successful in 1972. Following a decade of political frustration, commitment for adoption of a statewide code was achieved during two sessions of the Virginia General Assembly, despite some well-circulated rumors that farmers would be told how to build chicken coops, and barns would have to be equipped with sprinklers.

Professional technical associations and historical and cultural interests exerted considerable influence toward the adoption of the legislation and as a result were well represented on the State Board of Housing charged by the general assembly in 1972 with the selection, refinement and phrasing of a code.

The Committee on Historic Resources of the Virginia Chapter of the American Institute of Architects and the Virginia State Landmarks Commission made simultaneous and specialized efforts to insure that preservation interests were fully reflected in the code. The influence of the Virginia Building Officials Conference was also significant. These officials, having been required to enforce their original codes and also to react rationally to the realities of cases brought before them, had long been concerned with the resulting dichotomy. In the late 1940s the author was invited to present a paper at the Virginia Building Officials annual meeting, a request repeated in 1972 when state building code was a political issue. These officials emphasized the need for special regulations for historic structures, regulations that would be uncompromising with respect to public safety and liability but would also reflect the concern they felt for the validity and essential value of preservation efforts in Virginia.

The Code

The recommended code of the Building Official and Code Administrators, International (BOCA) was adopted as the basic uniform statewide building code in 1972. The legislation added several administrative amendments, none altering the goal of uniformity and simplification of code compliance. Section 318.0, Special Historic Buildings and Districts, is an amendment of particular interest to preservationists.

Some Results

The experiences of preservationists and architects in operating under this new code were surveyed by the author, who asked more than 50 leading architects and engineers in Virginia to share their experiences. Reports indicated that the greatest relief came not to the architects but to the building officials, who had long maintained a tolerant and liberal interpretation of the codes. However, liberal interpretation had been made with misgivings and, what is more important, with an awareness of potential official liability for catastrophes. The replies indicated an unexpected simplification; although the state code provides for a review board to make amending adjustments, no cases had been referred to the review board as of early 1974. Local building officials appear to be strengthened in their routine judgments by the phrasing of section 318 ". . . buildings are judged by the building official to be safe and in the public's interest, health, safety and welfare. . . ." The officials are now utilizing the judgmental latitude explicit in the code and are now doing legally many of the things they in the past did with sympathetic understanding but with questionable legality.

An Example

An example of how the code is working and of the simplification made possible by the code is offered by an experience with the stabilization and restoration of a historical house proposed for adaptive use as a museum and cultural center. Architects candidly listed every code violation and imaginable hazard and requested a meeting with the local building official. The official assembled a conference with key staff decision-makers and the architect's staff. The first action of the

JEFFERSON HOTEL (1895), *Richmond, Va. (Virginia Historic Landmarks Commission)*

Stearns Iron Front Building *(c. 1865-69), Richmond, Va. Cast-iron row structure. (Wm. Edmund Barrett for Virginia Historic Landmarks Commission)*

meeting was to define the status of the building; it had been classified by the local Historical Commission and the State Landmarks Commission as a historic building, an important fact and a key element in interpretation of the code. The official then assumed administrative authority and responsibility as provided in the code, eliminating referral to the state review board. Each of the staff then reviewed the tentative documents presented in accordance with their particular disciplines and responsibilities.

The meeting lasted a little more than an hour and resulted in approvals and decisions that would have easily taken months of correspondence, negotiation and uncertain liabilities otherwise.

Legislation encouraging reasonable code provisions for the preservation of historic structures can be achieved more easily at the state than at the local level. However, Virginia has enacted a viable precedent and is seeking to have section 318.0 become an integral part of the national codes.

A Uniform Statewide Building Code with Provisions for Historic Buildings and Districts: The Code Official's View

WILLIAM G. WHARTON

William G. Wharton, PE, is a consultant with the Virginia Office of Housing. He was formerly commissioner of buildings in Richmond, Va. He is past president of the Richmond Chapter, Building Officials Conference of America, and of the Building Officials Conference in Virginia.

The 1972 Virginia General Assembly passed legislation creating a State Board of Housing and directed it to adopt a building code that would apply equally across Virginia. On January 29, 1973, the State Board of Housing selected a nationally recognized, performance-oriented code. Using the model code of Building Officials and Code Administrators, International (BOCA), as a basis, the Board adopted the following as the Uniform Statewide Building Code of Virginia, to become effective September 1, 1973: The BOCA Basic Building Code/1970 with Accumulative Supplement 1972; BOCA Basic Mechanical Code/1971; BOCA Basic Plumbing Code 1970 with Accumulative Supplement 1972; One and Two Family Dwelling Code, 1971 Edition; and National Electric Code 1971 and excerpts for One and Two Family Dwellings, Virginia Administrative Amendments/1973 (changes that were required for the adopted model code to conform to the Legislative Enabling Act).

The Virginia General Assembly also created a Board of State Building Code Review (the Review Board) to interpret provisions of the code, to hear appeals and to grant temporary extensions to municipalities for the continued use of existing codes. The extensions were needed to provide for an orderly transfer of administrative requirements.

Since the adoption of the basic code on January 29, 1973, the State Board of Housing has updated the Uniform Statewide Building Code by adoption of the following: BOCA Basic Plumbing Code Accumulative Supplement 1972; One and Two Family Dwelling Code Accumulative Supplement 1973; and Updated Administrative Amendments.

One of the administrative amendments to the Uniform Statewide Building Code established a precedent in building codes in the United States by providing regulations for the preservation and restoration of historic buildings and districts. Many municipalities have adopted local ordinances providing means for the preservation of these historical resources, but these provisions had never before been included in a building code.

The section added to the basic code by the Review Board is as follows:

Section 318.0 Special Historic Buildings and Districts

> The provisions of the Basic Code, relating to the construction, repair, alteration, enlargement, restoration and moving of buildings or structures identified and classified by the State and/or local government authority as Historic Buildings subject to approval of the Review Board when such buildings are judged by the building official to be safe and in the public's interest of health, safety and welfare regarding any proposed construction, alteration, repair, enlargement, relocation, and location within fire districts. All such approvals must be based on the applicant's complete submission of professional architectural and engineering plans and specifications bearing the professional seal of the designer.

It is an established fact that a building code shall prescribe standards to be complied with in the construction of a building and that the provisions thereof shall be such as to protect the health, safety and welfare of the public. Section 318.0 provides this protection and also provides for the preservation of historic buildings with professional approval.

The engineering design of a building depends largely upon the proposed use of the building and in what fire or zoning district it is located or is to be located. The local municipalities will have to approve variances in these local requirements before they reach the Review Board.

The Uniform Statewide Building Code has not been in operation long enough to evaluate section 318.0; in fact, up to this time no case has come before the Review Board, but it does not mean that historic preservation is not taking place in the state. Some of it may be taking place under permits issued on plans completed before September 1, 1973, and others may be approved by municipalities that were granted a one-year extension by the Review Board for the use of codes in existence at the time of the approval of the basic code on September 1, 1973.

Section 318.0 has been discussed with the Office of the Historic Landmarks Commission of Virginia, Colonial Williamsburg Restoration Authorities and the Department of Planning of the City of Richmond in reference to St. John's Church Historical Area, and they all seem to be satisfied with it and think that it will meet their needs.

CITY HALL, *Alexandria, Va. Conference participants tour City Hall, in Alexandria Historic District. (Carleton Knight, III — National Trust)*

Case Studies of Building Code Problems for Preservation Projects in Alexandria, Va.

BAIRD M. SMITH

Baird M. Smith is a graduate architect with J. Everette Fauber, Jr., FAIA, Architect, in Alexandria, Va. He was employed by the Department of Field Services of the National Trust to plan the Preservation and Building Codes conference.

Alexandria, Va., in 1946 officially established a program to protect its architectural heritage by creating a historic district in Old Town, encompassing more than 50 blocks of 18th and 19th-century buildings. Ordinance 984 established a Board of Architectural Review consisting of three licensed architects, a real estate broker and five others who have demonstrated interest in the historical character of Old Town. No new construction or remodeling can proceed without board review and approval of facade design, materials, signs and automobile and pedestrian traffic, to name a few controls.

The architectural firm of J. Everette Fauber, Jr., FAIA, was selected by the Northern Virginia Regional Park Authority in 1972 to restore the John Carlyle House and to prepare a research program for the restoration of the Bank of Alexandria. The Alexandria City Council selected the firm to restore Gadsby's Tavern. Nathaniel P. Neblett, architectural historian, is in charge of all three of the Alexandria projects.* C. Richard Bierce, resident architect in Alexandria, is in charge of the firm's field office. As a staff member, I have provided the following on how the firm has attempted to solve code problems in these three buildings. These projects are subject to the regulations of the Basic Building Code, 1970 Edition, of the Building Officials and Code Administrators, International, with Commonwealth of Virginia and City of Alexandria amendments.

Gadsby's Tavern

Gadsby's Tavern is currently in the preliminary design stages; proposals have been formulated for the restoration. The project includes three different, but connected, structures. The three-story building (c. 1770) is the City Tavern. In 1792, John Wise built the main four-story building, which John Gadsby operated for a decade as the City Hotel. The rear, two-story structure was built in the 1870s and is currently occupied by the American Legion.

The Fauber firm has been commissioned to research and document the architectural history of the three buildings, to provide modern kitchen and mechanical facilities for an 18th-century-style tavern and restaurant, to provide complete environmental and fire protection systems for the complex and to provide modern club and meeting rooms for the American Legion post. The City Tavern and the second floor of the City Hotel will continue as museum display spaces. The basement and first floor of the City Hotel will house the kitchen and working tavern facilities.

At the outset of the project, it was obvious that stairways and fire exits were a major problem. All three buildings are considered places of public assembly. The City Tavern had a central, open wood stair. The City Hotel, the main four-story building, also had only a central, open wood stair. The attached American Legion wing had no stair but shared that of the City Hotel. A four-story smoke tower will be provided near the center of the complex, with a second two-story smoke tower at the west end of the American Legion wing. The central smoke tower is inside the existing building, but the west stair tower is attached to the exterior of the existing building and poses the challenge of creating a compatible design.*

Even with the addition of these stairs there would not be two exits from every public space because the second and third floors of the City Tavern still would have only the original wood stair. Also, the upper floors of City Hotel would have only one fully complying fire exit, and this exit would be compromised because the existing wood stair is adjacent to it and a fire in the stair would block access to the fire exit. The firm's current solution to these problems includes a variety of measures: The wall that now separates the two second floor spaces will be penetrated with two fire doors, allowing exit in opposite directions. Similar changes will be made on the third floor. The fourth floor of the City Hotel will not be open to the public. It will, however, house air conditioning equipment.

These solutions to the fire exit problems work in conjunction with an elaborate fire protection system. A system to detect heat and smoke works in combination with an extinguishing system of Halon gas in the City Tavern, and with a water sprinkler system in all the other public spaces, to provide a complete

*Nathaniel P. Neblett is currently restoration architect with the National Trust for Historic Preservation. — ed.

*At Gadsby's Tavern, smoke towers were not required to comply with exit requirements. Interior exitways were substituted. — ed.

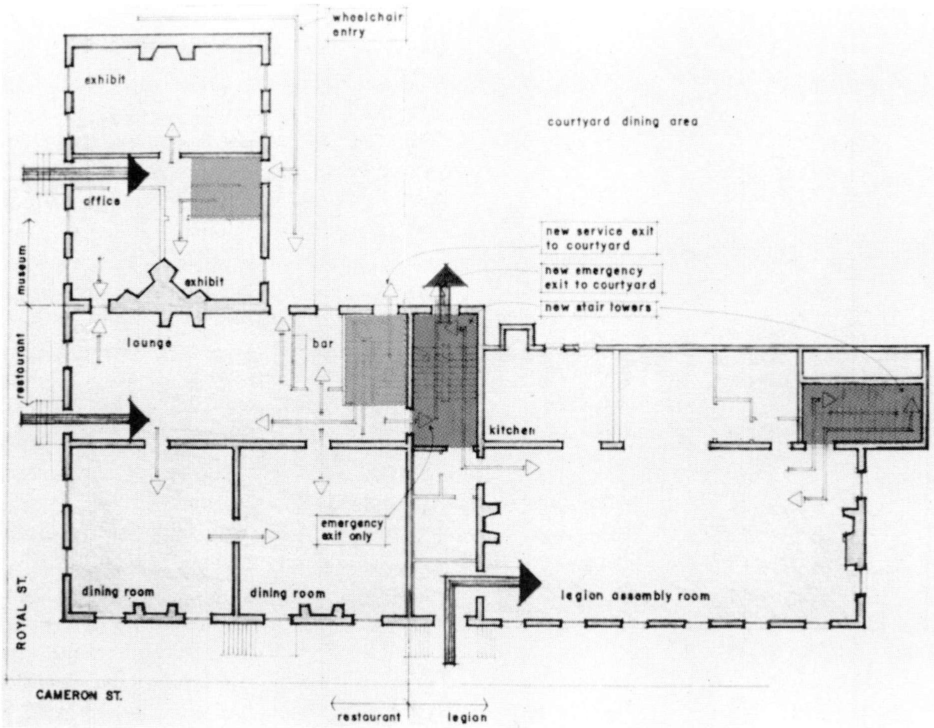

GADSBY'S TAVERN *first floor circulation plan (above). Tavern (top); hotel (center); American Legion wing (right). New fire exits (dark shading); existing open stairs (light shading). (J. Everette Fauber, Jr., FAIA) City Tavern (c. 1770) (left) and City Hotel (1792) (right), Alexandria, Va. Restored for use as museum, meeting rooms and tavern. (Fauber)*

fire protection system. In addition, a water curtain, or deluge system, will be installed in the City Hotel around the original open stair to insure access to the adjoining fire exit.*

John Carlyle House

The John Carlyle House, built in 1752, is an important mid-century Virginia mansion. Carlyle bought two pieces of Alexandria property in 1749 and erected this stone house, one of the first in the city. The City Hall, or Courthouse, was always located immediately opposite this house. The house is somewhat peculiar in that it is and was a mansion of basically rural design, with dependencies, placed in an urban setting. After Carlyle built this house, Alexandria passed an ordinance stating that all houses had to be built in the townhouse, adjoining partywall, style.

The firm's project is to restore Carlyle House, now owned by the Northern Virginia Regional Park Authority, to its 1752 character to become a house museum. This project includes extensive research, both archaeological and documentary, to be followed by a restoration feasibility study. The firm is currently preparing the contract documents for the restoration.

Of critical importance to code compliance at Carlyle House was an early decision by the local building code official. For strict compliance to the building code, the house museum should have been classified as a place of public assembly, necessitating compliance with rigid regulations. The code official determined that, as a historic house museum, with controlled public access and a sophisticated fire protection system, the regulations for a building of public assembly would not have to be rigidly followed. The code official and the architect worked together, on a case-by-case basis, to bring the house to a condition safe for the public.

The house is built on a central hall plan, with two rooms on each side of the main hall. Only one stair descends to the basement. This service stair was used for servant access from the basement to the dining room above and on up to the second and third floor bedrooms. It was taken out in the mid-19th century but will now be put back. The local code official wanted the entire stair, from basement to attic, to meet requirements for one-hour fire-rated construction. The architects preferred using historical materials where the service stair adjoined museum spaces. As a compromise, one-hour fire-rated construction was required only in the basement portion of the stair. The code official also allowed beaded boards to be placed over the fire-rated construction to correspond with the adjoining surface treatments. The original central stair will be reproduced to replace the existing Victorian period stair. This open, wood stair will serve the first and second floors.

The entire house will have a Halon fire extinguishing system. This odorless, colorless, liquified gas extinguishes fire by chemically interfering with the combustion process. Each room will have concealed heat detectors that work in conjunction with smoke detectors located in each return air duct. If smoke is detected, an alarm is sounded. If heat is detected in one of four zones, all nozzles in that zone discharge. The four Halon zones in the house will be created by designating certain doors as control doors. These doors are held open by an electromagnetic catch that releases when heat is detected in that zone. The doors in museum spaces will be closed by reproduced 18th-century wrought iron spring closers. Doors in other spaces will have modern closers concealed below the flooring. All heat detectors and spray nozzles will be concealed behind cornices or door trims.

Emergency lighting, with battery pack floodlights, would normally have been required. At Carlyle House, however, an auxiliary electric circuit connects selected light fixtures in the side corridors and central hall. The architect desired to eliminate electric lights in this 18th-century setting, but the safety of house staff and visitors dictated the need for emergency lighting. The need for lighted exit signs was waived. The code official will accept signs painted in subtle colors and placed on each of the major exit doors.

Handicapped persons will have access to the first floor; an exterior automated lift will be provided adjacent to the south entry. The first floor is about four

*Since the conference presentation, many changes in code compliance have occurred at Gadsby's Tavern.

The use of Halon gas in the City Tavern was abandoned in favor of a common water sprinkler system throughout the project. Each sprinkler head is independent of any other and activates only when the temperature at the head rises above 140°F. The fire detection system has also been updated. Manual pull-stations and smoke detectors in return air ducts and in the open wood stairs, when activated, will sound an alarm that should allow all persons in the building to exit safely.

It was only after the fire protection system was refined to this degree that the code official allowed several variances from the building code. The plan for a water curtain or deluge system at the original City Hotel stair was also abandoned. Instead, smoke detectors were placed at this stair to insure an immediate alarm should fire occur.

The requirement for two fire doors between the second floor spaces was reduced to one door, properly marked as an exit. The direction of door swing was determined by establishing which space would have the largest number of people. On the third floor it became physically impossible to provide a second exit from either the City Tavern or the City Hotel. The code official, realizing the waste of usable space if the third floor were closed to use, decided to allow controlled and restricted use in these spaces. The third floor of the City Hotel will be office space for the museum and restaurant staffs. The third floor of the City Tavern will continue to display bedrooms, but will have limited access by the public. — ed.

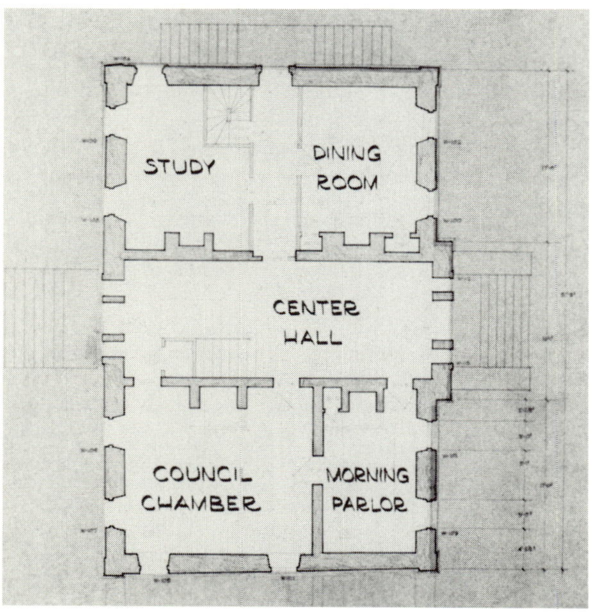

CARLYLE HOUSE *(1752), Alexandria, Va. Sketch of restoration plan (above) and first floor plan. (Fauber)*

feet above the outside grade. Rather than ramps up to the front or side entries, the power lift was chosen because it was less disruptive to the aesthetic balance of the front facade.

BANK OF ALEXANDRIA BUILDING

The Bank of Alexandria was built in 1804 by Carlyle's son-in-law as combined bank and living quarters for bank employees. By the mid-19th century a four-story wing had been added to the original three-story bank. The bank and wing were used as a hotel and later as an apartment building until the present time. This enlarged building, the Braddock House Hotel, almost completely surrounded the Carlyle House.

The firm was commissioned by the owner to do archaeological and documentary research on the bank. Restoration of the bank building is contemplated, but work has not begun toward the restoration. The project is included here to illustrate what code compliance problems an architect faces at the beginning of a project.

The building is three stories high with an attic and is of masonry bearing wall construction with heavy timber framing. The only stair is of central,

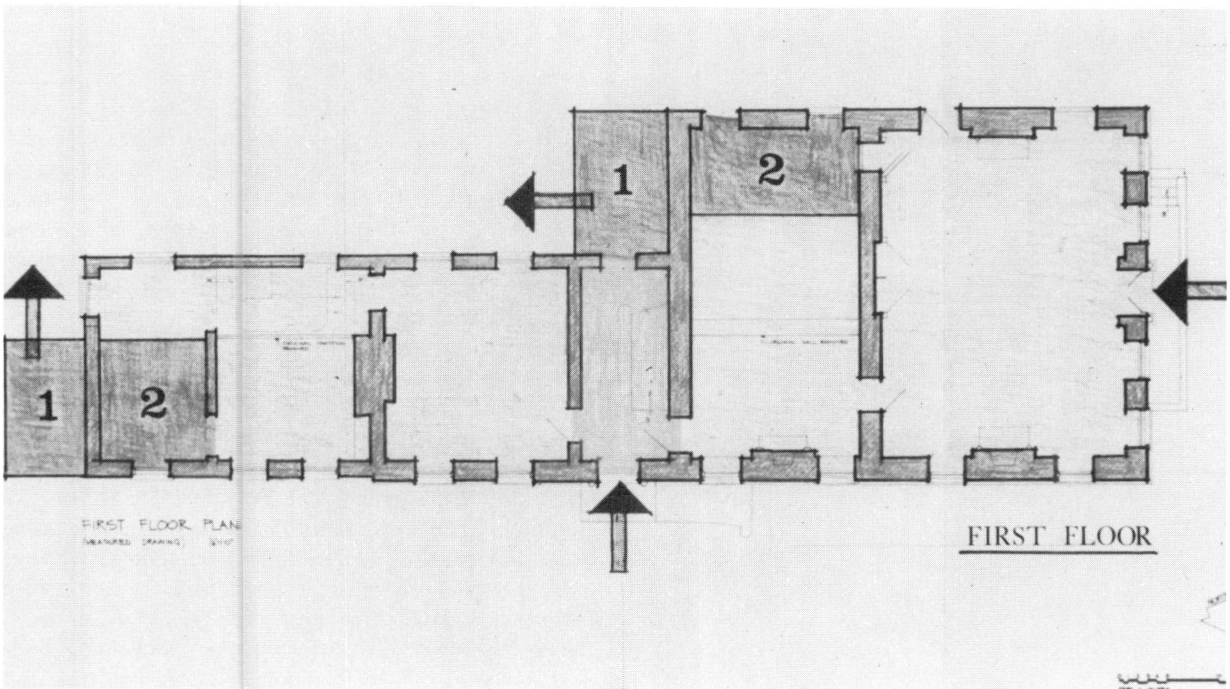

Bank of Alexandria (1804), *Alexandria, Va. View of 1804 structure (above); first floor plan. Proposed stairs and elevator locations numbered 1 and 2. (Fauber)*

open, wood construction. It is assumed that the building will be used for public assembly and might include shops and offices.

In examining possible locations for stairs and elevators, it becomes evident that providing enough safe exits from the upper floors would be difficult. In addition, one would have to decide whether to place the stair towers outside the building, creating an aesthetic problem, or to place them inside the building, using rentable floor space.

Any and all variances to the building code are possible only through a case-by-case analysis of each problem. Ingenuity and aggressiveness of the architect must be matched with open-mindedness of the code official.

Discussion

Comments made by the speakers and the audience during the discussion of current solutions are here summarized.

In New Orleans the board of building planners and appeals is a legal interpreter of the building codes. It also has the right of waiver. The board consists of an architect, a civil engineer, a mechanical engineer and representatives of a local insurance agency and a local construction firm. The appeal costs $50, and the decision is binding. When the board receives an appeal, it is placed on the docket according to the date it was filed. Appeals are not segregated into types. The board meets regularly every month. Legally, the board is limited to a specified number of meetings. The board circumvents this limitation by recessing and reconvening a few days later, depending on the nature and volume of the case.

The board has wide latitude, and its authority has held up well in court decisions. The New Orleans code states that the decisions of the board cannot be reversed by the city council; only the court can reverse a board decision. The only adverse court decision to date involved a red fence between two properties. The court stated that the board can waive anything except the property boundaries. The property rights of the neighbor must be taken into consideration.

There are two ways to deal with an unsatisfactory building code regulation. Either change the regulation or seek some kind of waiver through an appeals board such as the one in New Orleans. Construction materials businesses do not hesitate to try to change requirements, but designers and preservationists seem willing to take the less creative route by seeking individual waivers, which means that subsequent appeals must go through the same route. Both routes, changing the standard and seeking the waiver, are open to historic preservationists and designers.

Nine out of 10 architects are indifferent to building code regulations. They think codes are a nuisance and interfere with their practices. Architects are not aggressive about getting regulations changed. Few architects are attending the hearings of the Southern Building Code Conference. The number of architects that propose changes is even less. Many architects who attend the hearings believe they are not knowledgeable enough to propose changes. It is the architects' fault that the codes are not changed; they do not participate actively enough in the code change process. Architects will attend a preservation conference like this one and complain, but they stay away from building code hearings.

National Code Organizations

Historic Preservation and the Basic Building Code

LEO J. CANTOR, PE

Leo J. Cantor, PE, is commissioner of buildings in Richmond, Va. He has been chairman of the Interpretations and Code Changes Committees of the Building Officials and Code Administrators, International.

The original Building Officials and Code Administrators (BOCA) Basic Building Code of 1950 gave early recognition to the exceptional situation of building construction that does not lend itself to exact compliance with code requirements. Latitude was provided by including the following code sections: section 106.0, Existing Buildings; section 110.0, Modifications; section 128.0, Board of Appeals.

These sections have been retained in each subsequent edition of the BOCA Basic Code up to and including the present 1970 edition as amended in 1973. A review of these sections discloses the particular flexibility each affords to code deviation. The section dealing with Existing Buildings, section 106.0, allows restoration of structures, with the same kind of materials contained in the building, of up to 25 percent of the physical value of the building. If the extent of repair and renovation exceeds 25 percent but is less than 50 percent, the building official is given the authority to determine the required degree and extent of exact code compliance with the implication as well of the degree of noncompliance. It is axiomatic that section 106.0 applies to existing occupancies. Should there be an intent to change use or occupancy, then those portions affected must subscribe to the current code requirements. However, in the case of the typical small house museum restoration, the residential occupancy classification is not considered to be altered unless the projected occupancy will exceed 100. In such cases, the building must fulfill all the code requirements of a place of assembly. When alterations exceed 50 percent of the physical value of the structure or involve increased size or height, exact code compliance is mandatory.

To answer those special problems that are not within the scope of section 106.0, section 110.0, Modifications, is another available procedure:

> When there are practical difficulties involved in carrying out structural or mechanical provisions of the Basic Code or of an approved rule, the building official may vary or modify such provision upon application of the owner or his representative, provided that the spirit and intent of the law shall be observed and public welfare and safety be assured. The application for modification and the final decision of the building official shall be in writing and shall be officially recorded with the application for the permit and the permanent records of the Department of Building Inspection.

This performance requirement couples a mechanism for resolution with an obligation to fully document the reasons for the action taken. The requirement of written documentation safeguards against any surreptitious act by either the applicant or the official by making the record available to public examination. This provision is particularly suited for use in major restoration or alteration of historic buildings. Such buildings were constructed under earlier criteria, and not only has technology changed, but the site and environment have changed. For example, a historic building located within the central business district (CBD) of any major city is usually within a fire district number 1 that does not allow type 3C (exterior masonry walls with wood structural members) or 4 (frame construction) buildings. These types of historic buildings within the central business district run into code conflict if restoration for more than 25-50 percent of physical value is attempted. Under section 110.0 the designer has the option to propose alternate solutions to code requirements that cannot accommodate structural and mechanical systems of the historic building.

For example, installing special fire detection and suppression systems can compensate for the use of combustible components. Section 110.0 does not specifically deny the possibility of a change of use or occupancy, so it is possible to obtain such a change if the requirements of section 110.0 are met.

The last option available for variation from strict code compliance is the Board of Appeals process, section 128.0.

In the case of a historic building restoration involving either the replacement of a recently gutted or destroyed structure or the new construction of a structure as a result of a particular civic interest action, the work involves a complete new construction that would not fall within either of the described procedures for existing buildings or for modifications; consideration for code variation could only be sought under the Board of Appeals process. Within section 128.0 three appeal situations are recognized: (1) "true intent of the Basic Code or the rules legally adopted thereunder have been incorrectly interpreted," (2) "the provisions of the Basic Code do not apply," (3) "an equally good or better form of construction can be used." The last of these alternate claims allows the employment of innovative architectural and engineering solutions in overcoming code constraints that may inhibit historic building restoration.

Although these procedures have been available for historical restoration, there had previously been no special focus on historic preservation in the BOCA code, but as the emphasis on historic preservation increased nationwide, stimulated by the Civil War Centennial and the anticipated national Bicentennial, there was a need to develop more direct code application to such construction. In response to this need the BOCA committee for recommending code changes, the Basic Code Committee, proposed a code change in 1974, section 318.0, Special Historic Buildings and Districts. The section allows a professional designer to propose construction procedures irrespective of exact code requirements, provided public health, safety and welfare are safeguarded. Section 318.0 is intended to allow a direct and uniform policy by minimizing the subjective appraisals of regulatory officials and by declaring the right for historic preservation to claim variance rather than to obtain variance by the grant of a special privilege. The code change was publicly presented at the regularly scheduled BOCA Basic Code Change hearings in Fort Lauderdale, Fla. in January 1974. The text of the change was patterned after a recently adopted technical statutory requirement of the Virginia Uniform Statewide Building Code. Section 318.0 drew the support of the National Trust for Historic Preservation through the testimony of Baird Smith. After the hearings, the BOCA Basic Code Change Committee recommended approval of the change. Since the January 1974 hearing it has been discovered that an inadvertent inclusion in section 318.0 places responsibility for the classification of the historical nature of a structure on the building official. This was not the intent of the section; I was party to offering the original regulation in the Virginia code and also a member of the BOCA Basic Code Committee that sponsored the change. Therefore, I propose to offer an editorial amendment to the present BOCA change scheduled for final adoption at the code changes hearing at the BOCA Annual Convention in Detroit in June 1974. The following draft with proposed editorial corrections does not substantially alter the original code change (the changed text is in italics):

> *Section 318.0, Special Historic Buildings and Districts* The provisions of the Basic Code, relating to the construction, repair, alteration, enlargement, restoration and moving of buildings or structures shall not be mandatory for existing buildings or structures identified and classified by the *state and/or local government authority* as Historic Buildings subject to the approval of the Board of Appeals when such buildings are judged by the building official to be safe and in the public's interest of health, safety and welfare regarding any proposed construction, alteration, repair, enlargement, relocation, and location within fire districts. All such approvals must be based on the applicant's complete submission of professional architectural and engineering plans and specifications bearing the professional seal of the designer.

The code change process incorporated into the BOCA program allows for and encourages continued updating of the BOCA Basic Code. Sponsors may submit changes to the BOCA organization for consideration with supporting statements. These are distributed to the BOCA membership prior to a public hearing held in January each year. At this time sponsors, proponents, opponents or interested citizens offer verbal or written statements regarding the code change to the BOCA Code Change Committee, which presides over an assembly of building officials, professionals, industrial representatives and others.

After the public hearing is completed, testimony and written submissions are reviewed and evaluated by the Code Change Committee. The committee then determines a recommendation on the change and a reason for the recommendation, to be distributed to the membership prior to the BOCA Annual Convention held the following June. The code changes are again heard in public assembly at the convention, with additional testimony and amendments taken and the change voted upon by the membership. This due process system for code changes is deemed the most democratic and complete review procedure of any code promulgating body.

Although building codes often have been stereotyped as archaic, restrictive or unresponsive, BOCA has exemplified the converse by promoting flexible, performance-oriented code provisions as well as by initiating code changes for code improvement. Typical of BOCA policy is advocacy of section 318.0 Special Historic Districts and Buildings as represented by the actions of the Basic Code Committee, the Basic Building Code Changes Committee and ultimately by rank and file membership, which is expected to endorse and vote for the adoption of the amended code change at the Annual Convention in June 1974.*

*The amended code change was endorsed and adopted on June 11, 1974, at the BOCA Annual Convention. — ed.

Historic Buildings and the Uniform Building Code

ROBERT E. O'BANNON

Robert E. O'Bannon is director of education for the International Conference of Building Officials. He is active in developing plans for improving the training of building department personnel and is the author of Building Department Administration.

The Uniform Building Code is the principal product of the International Conference of Building Officials, an association composed of building officials from villages, townships, cities and counties in 44 states. The code was formulated in 1927, culminating a five-year effort initiated by 13 West Coast building officials in 1922. The philosophy of the code writers, "to provide a maximum of safety at a minimum of cost," has been maintained through the years and is a reflection of the principle of police power from which such codes derive their authority.

The primary purpose of any regulatory code is to provide reasonable safeguards for the protection of the life, health and safety of the public, safeguarding it from dangers that might otherwise be present in buildings and structures or, more appropriate to the theme of historic preservation, from inadequate or improper maintenance.

The first model code, the National Building Code of the National Board of Fire Underwriters, appeared in 1905. The code was sponsored by the Casualty Insurance Underwriters, which was concerned predominantly with property loss. Primary users were smaller political subdivisions that had neither the resources nor the capability of independently developing and maintaining a building code, while collectively they could and did maintain a code. This collective effort still provides the basis for the democratic and continuous code change process, a necessary counterpart to the dynamic nature of construction.

Just What is a Historic Building?

Obviously, a precise definition would be difficult to develop because there are so many variables. Apparently the various state statutes that provide for the preservation of historic landmarks reflect this problem because they are somewhat loosely worded and nondefinitive, requiring value judgments by those to whom the task of identification and preservation is assigned. Each committee, commission or department operating under the authority of a statute or ordinance develops its own parameters for identification of historic monuments and procedures for their preservation.

There is an unfortunate opinion, held by many uninformed persons, that old buildings, having survived the ravages of time, have been endowed with immortality and are thus indestructible. A sad fact of life is that, due to their age and condition, they are usually unsafe. If a building has been declared to have historical significance and the public is to be encouraged to visit it, it must be made reasonably safe. But some purists display reluctance to take any type of corrective action, even to components that are not readily discernible and to changes that will have no aesthetic effect, such as the electrical system, which in older buildings is often seriously deficient.

Building Code Compliance

At first glance the building code might seem to be the primary adversary of old buildings, and the objectives of preservationists and code administrators might seem to be opposed. But upon close examination of the code it can be seen that, although there is no specific mention of historic buildings, they are protected. The code even provides means for the repair or restoration of historic buildings as an alternative to destruction.

Section 104(g) states: "Buildings in existence at the time of the passage of this code may have their existing use or occupancy continued, if such use or occupancy was legal at the time of the passage of this code, provided such continued use is not dangerous to life." This means that if a building has been adequately maintained and its authorized use has not been changed, compliance with current code requirements is not necessary. Compliance is necessary with a change of occupancy or when a building is found to be unsafe. When evaluating an older structure for a change in use, it should be considered as having characteristics that are a threat to life, health and safety until a thorough investigation has either disproved or confirmed the presence of dangers.

Change of occupancy, often a major problem, is currently exemplified by the conversion of older buildings to use as tourist attractions in some major cities. Some of these conversions are being made without regard to two of the code's major concerns: fire and life safety and structural stability.

If the building has changed from a lesser to a more restricted use, the building official has no alternative other than to insist on compliance with code requirements for the new use. This does not mean that corrective action must necessarily disfigure, destroy or even interfere with any aesthetic or historical qualities; these can in most cases be preserved. The Hearst Castle at San Simeon, Calif., is a good example of a nondisfiguring alteration in which additional exit facilities were installed to accommodate the large numbers of persons who would be visiting the mansion.

An unsafe building is one that has, through age, lack of maintenance or misuse, developed characteristics that are threats to life, health or safety. But these conditions seldom constitute justification for immediate demolition. When dealing with an unsafe building, the building official must initiate whatever action is deemed necessary to first neutralize and then abate the hazard. Section 203 of the Uniform Building Code includes provisions for repair or rehabilitation as an alternative to demolition or removal of an unsafe structure. When a building has suffered damage to the extent that the wreckage is manifestly unsafe, and if the danger is sufficiently grave to require immediate remedial action, the building official may have no choice other than to exercise the authority for summary abatement and order immediate demolition. This drastic action is seldom taken, for a number of reasons, but the authority and responsibility for demolition are inherent in the position of the person responsible for code enforcement. The building official is often in the unenviable position of playing devil's advocate. Taking action against an old, possibly revered, structure is one of those times, but irrespective of personal feeling, public safety is the primary responsibility of the building official.

Any action taken by a building official requires rigid adherence to the constitutional protection guaranteeing legal due process. This process includes providing for public hearings, taking sworn testimony and presentation of credible evidence. Initially this hearing may be before the appeals board, established by section 204 of the Uniform Building Code. This board is empowered to make reasonable interpretations of the code, including overruling a decision of the building official. If it is the board decision that a building must be altered or changed in the interest of public safety, the matter can still be referred to the courts for relief. These are the legal safeguards intended to prevent arbitrary actions against private property as guaranteed by the Fourth Amendment of the U.S. Constitution.

Aside from the appeal process, mechanisms within the code offer other alternatives and solutions for reasonable code compliance for older structures. For example, portions of section 104 of the Uniform Building Code contain provisions pertaining to existing structures. These provisions set forth varying requirements for repairs, including the utilization of materials of which the building was originally constructed. The imposition of code requirements depends on the amount of work to be done expressed as a percentage of the building valuation, meaning current replacement cost. These provisions are not generous concessions, but they can be used for total restoration over a period of time, provided the occupancy has not been affected. In those areas of the country where earthquakes are probable, there is particular and legitimate concern over the structural stability of older buildings, but even in these areas restoration has been accomplished by using the original building materials, while insuring structural integrity by installing necessary components to resist lateral forces.

The Uniform Building Code does have provisions for preservation, but perhaps they are too obscure and sophisticated for easy application. There may be a need to clearly delineate and provide for those buildings and structures that have, by competent authority, been declared to have historical or architectural significance and thus reduce the chances of their loss through condemnation and demolition. But an unqualified immunity provision is not the answer. Because the procedural maintenance of the Uniform Building Code adheres steadfastly to democratic principles, anyone may submit recommendations for changes which, if approved, will appear in the subsequent issue. The preparation and submission of a reasonable and realistic code amendment might be a task for the National Trust for Historic Preservation.*

*See Appendix A for Section 203 (j) Historic Buildings, of the Uniform Building Code, adopted in 1975 after supportive testimony from Melvyn Green on behalf of the National Trust. — ed.

Historic Buildings and the National Building Code

DARIO L. CONTE-RUSSIAN

Dario L. Conte-Russian is involved in code work and fire protection engineering with the American Insurance Association. He formerly served as assistant to the vice president, Utility Division, Vollmer Associates.

The decision of whether or not a building should be officially classified as a historic building generally rests with the state or local jurisdiction. The basis for evaluation is primarily architectural, and the designation generally denotes a building that has a special historical and aesthetic interest and value and that represents a period or style of architecture typical of an era in United States history.

After a building has been classified as historic, building code officials are faced with the task of determining whether or not the building is reasonably safe to persons and property and, if not, what alterations are necessary to render it safe without disturbing building characteristics that should be preserved.

Provisions of the 1967 edition of the National Building Code, although they do not include specific requirements on historic buildings, may be interpreted to apply to historic buildings the provisions for existing buildings and for buildings that are converted from one occupancy classification to another. Specific provisions for historic buildings are planned for the next edition of the National Building Code and are being developed at the present time, but cannot be presented now because they have not been finalized.*

It is necessary to differentiate between buildings that have the same type of occupancy they had before they were officially classified as historic buildings and buildings that are converted from one occupancy classification to another after they are classified as historic buildings.

Article XVII, Requirements for Existing Buildings

Historic buildings with no changes of occupancy must conform within a reasonable time (as determined by a written order of the building official) to the provisions of article XVII, Requirements for Existing Buildings. Except for minor sections that apply to interior finish, roof covering repairs, chimneys and vents, determination of floor loads, heat producing appliances and plumbing, article XVII deals with means of egress in buildings of all types of occupancy except dwellings and farm buildings. Of major importance is the requirement that every story with an occupant load of 50 or more persons have two separate exits. However, except for educational and institutional occupancies, a single exit may be used for stories having fewer than 100 occupants when stairways or other floor openings are enclosed by construction having a fire resistance rating of not less than one hour. This exception only applies to buildings of fire-resistive construction, buildings of other than fire-resistive construction not more than two stories in height and buildings equipped with approved automatic sprinkler systems. In historic buildings having any type of occupancy—except for assembly occupancy, which is permitted an increase of 50 feet, and business occupancy, which is not permitted any increase—travel distances to the nearest exit are allowed to be 25 feet greater than the travel distance requirements for new construction. As with new construction, in buildings equipped with approved automatic sprinkler systems or of either fire-resistive or noncombustible types of construction, occupied exclusively by stocks of noncombustible material, not packed or crated in combustible material, travel distances to the nearest exit are allowed to be 50 percent greater than the travel distance requirements for all other types of construction.

Article VI, Means of Egress

Historic buildings that are converted from one occupancy classification to another must conform to the provisions of article VI, Means of Egress. The conversion of a building into a museum from any other type of use, including that of a dwelling, or the opening of a building to the public while operations similar to the original uses are being performed is conversion to an assembly occupancy. Of major importance in article VI is the requirement that every story have no fewer than two separate exits. An exception, which must be pointed out because of the large number of historic buildings that are converted to museums, is that places of assembly with a capacity of fewer than 100 occupants are permitted to have only one exit, provided the place of assembly is located on a story at or near grade and the maximum distance from any point within the place of assembly to a doorway in an exterior wall does not exceed 50 feet.

In cases where code requirements appear to be too restrictive, detrimental to the appearance of a historic building or necessitating sacrifice of important architectural elements to meet such requirements, relief may be obtained by petitioning the board of appeal. The board of appeal may grant relief, provided it determines that safety to life will not be impaired or that alternate safety measures will result in equivalent safety to life.

*The 1975 edition of the National Building Code will include specific provisions for historic buildings and will be available for distribution in 1975. — ed.

For existing buildings, code provisions are primarily concerned with safety to life and in general are not concerned with potential property loss. Nevertheless, code provisions encourage the use of systems, equipment or assemblies to protect against property loss.

Summary

If there is no change of occupancy in a historic building, the National Building Code requires compliance only with the minimum standards for safety to life, a rather lenient approach. When a historic building is converted from one occupancy classification to another, the requirements for means of egress are the same as for new construction of that classification. Although the egress requirements may seem strict when applied to historic buildings, favorable decisions from the board of appeal in the special case of historic buildings may be expected to balance the general restrictions of the requirement.

The National Building Code recognizes the importance of trying to preserve historic buildings because of their intrinsic value and is aware of the need for building code provisions that will continue to provide safety to persons and property, while preserving these buildings to the fullest extent possible.

Discussion

Comments made by the speaker and the audience during the discussion of historic buildings and the National Building Code are here summarized.

In cases where the building code requirements appear to be too restrictive, relief may be sought by petitioning either the local or the state board of appeal. Relief may be sought directly from the state board for building, or structural, appeals. The uniform statewide building code does allow appeal of electrical and plumbing code requirements to go to a board composed of representatives from those professions: electrical engineers, architects and electrical contractors. When it is judged at the local level, the appeal must be filed with the state review board.

The fiscal value of a building as a determinant for the degree of performance of the code may be defined as assessed value, reconstruction value or appraised value. The fiscal value of a building, as interpreted in city ordinances of the National Building Code, is the value that is established by the city assessor. The assessor is charged by the legislative body to evaluate a building according to its actual sale value, including both the value of the land and the value of the building. A building that is 100 years old has usually suffered some depreciation.

Under the New Orleans Building Code, the fiscal value of historic buildings is interpreted as "replacement value." A structure with a replacement value of $50,000 will have a greater value after $100,000 of restoration work. When a preservation group begins a restoration project, it can usually depend on increasing the value of its building. This gives the restoration group a big break in the project's relation to code provisions concerning fiscal value.

The existing building constraint is directed toward any building that is uncompliant and unconforming to the building code. That constraint of 25 to 50 percent value is not intended to encourage the preservation of a dilapidated building that does not have any historical significance or to enable owners to circumvent new standards of safety and technology. This constraint provision in a code does not address itself only to restoration. The constraint is there to discourage the continuing practice of partially repairing dilapidated buildings instead of restoring them.

Under section 318.0, if a building official does not feel free to rule in favor of restoration the case is not automatically referred back to section 128, Board of Appeals. The opponent of preservation would have the right to raze the building.

There are now three options always available. The appeal procedure is still available; section 318.0 is an added option and if the building official does not like the idea of ruling on the basis of section 318.0, the appeal can be sent back to the appeals board.

Even when a building official rules on the basis of section 318.0, the appeal is filed with the review board. The reason for filing with the review board is that if some locality wanted to evade the state building code, all it would have to do is to declare the whole town a historic district.

Conversion of use does not entitle maintenance of a building according to code requirements for the previous use. Marshall House, which is used as a residence, cannot be indiscriminately converted to an office building disregarding building code requirements. However, under section 318.0, if there is professional evidence indicating that the John Marshall House can be adapted for use as an office building structurally, mechanically, electrically and in terms of means of egress, the Building Officials and Code Administrators will be able to approve the new use. Ownership of a building currently in use does not insure permission to adapt that building to a completely new use.

When fire-resistant materials cannot be used on the exterior of a building, other adaptations must be considered to produce the same fire rating. For example, a wood frame building located 30 feet from any other building has sufficient fire resistance. A highrise building was built next to the Robert E. Lee house near Richmond, Va., creating a code violation because the Lee house windows were not properly fire resistant due to proximity to the highrise. An exterior sprinkler system was installed.

Any BOCA member may also solicit an official code interpretation. Even that procedure is democratic; the code question is presented to a committee composed of representative officials from throughout the country, they reach a consensus on interpretation of the particular query and the interpretation is published.

Historic Preservation and the Southern Building Code Congress International

SAMUEL R. SPARKS

Samuel R. Sparks is director of advertising and promotion for the Southern Building Code Congress and editor of the SBCC Southern Building *magazine.*

One important consideration in any preservation endeavor is the particular building code in use and its relation to the project. At present, the Standard Codes promulgated by the Southern Building Code Congress International (SBCC) make no special provisions for preservation or restoration work on buildings of historical significance.

An obvious question is how preservation and restoration projects have been conducted under the Standard Codes if there are not special guidelines in the codes for such work. Like the other model codes, the Standard Codes serve as minimum standards for the local jurisdictions that adopt the codes and may be changed or amended by and for the local jurisdiction. Thus, a community and its government, desiring to make provisions for the preservation of either a historic area or a particular structure, may amend the code to provide for variances from it.

In addition to code changes on the local level, good communication and cooperation among architects, building officials and property owners are essential. In any preservation project, the architect has to understand not only the building official's position as enforcer of the code but also the basic purpose of the code. On the other hand, the building official has to make every effort to understand what is wanted and why it is wanted and then help the architect accomplish these plans under the local interpretation of the code.

Proposed Code Change

The SBCC is more than willing to make special provisions for historic preservation and restoration in its codes through the formal process of code revision. As with the other model code organizations, a code change has been submitted to the SBCC that, if adopted, would amend the Standard Code to give special consideration to historic buildings and districts. This proposed amendment would allow variances from the code as long as the building official judges such structures safe and that such variances would insure public health, safety and welfare.

This proposed amendment to the Standard Codes will be discussed at open committee hearings in June 1974 and will then be placed on the agenda of the SBCC Annual Research Conference in November 1974 for vote by the membership. If accepted, the provision would become effective in early 1975.*

An Example—Savannah, Ga.

There is no better example of historic preservation under the existing Standard Codes than the city of Savannah, Ga.

Savannah was founded in 1733 on the coast of Georgia by Gen. James Oglethorpe, an Englishman. Oglethorpe himself planned and supervised the construction of the first section of the city. The pattern for the inner city of present-day Savannah was set by the four original wards laid out by General Oglethorpe.

The Savannah National Historic Landmark District, 1966, is the largest urban historic district in the United States. In fact, 2½ square miles of old Savannah is a National Historic Landmark. Within the historic district are 1,100 structures of historical value; 850 of these are either restored, in the process of restoration or awaiting restoration.

The revitalization of the old section of Savannah began in the early 1940s. The effort has gained momentum and continues today, headed by a group of dedicated and energetic citizens. The people of Savannah have accomplished much through cooperation and communication among property owners, architects and the city Department of Inspections. Mires Rosenthal, Savannah director of inspections, explained the usual procedure in this way:

> The owners and architects come to us and show us what they want to do . . . then we try to show them how they can do it. We try to help in every way we can. Sometimes a few changes have to be made, sometimes none. We make allowances where we can. Our main concern is human safety.

Cooperation and communication have been and are the keys to any successful preservation project. When and if changes are made in the Standard Codes, making special provisions for historic preservation, the rapport between architect and building official will remain supremely important.

*The proposed amendment to the Standard Building Code, 103.4.1 Special Historic Buildings and Districts, was recommended for approval by the Standard Building Code Revision Committee. However, it was defeated on the floor at the 1974 Annual Research Conference in Birmingham, Ala. The prevalent reason given for opposition to the proposal was that building officials do not wish to be held responsible for injury and damage that may occur either directly or indirectly from allowed variance from the code. The same provision is to be reintroduced for consideration in 1975. — ed.

Application of the Life Safety Code to the Restoration and Use of Historic Buildings

H. H. SUMMERS, JR.

Howard H. Summers, Jr., is assistant chief fire marshal for Virginia and a member of the National Fire Protection Association.

A review of the model building codes, Southern, Building Officials and Code Administrators, Uniform and National, might lead one to the conclusion that historic buildings are not regulated by these codes. However, historic buildings are regulated. Where such buildings are not specifically included by type occupancy they would be included in the unclassified occupancy category. The Life Safety Code is no different from the other model codes in this respect. Historic buildings are not listed under any specific occupancy classifications in the Life Safety Code. They fall under section 4-120—Miscellaneous of chapter 4. Other chapters of the Life Safety Code may be applicable through this section. Of greatest importance is chapter 2—General (Fundamental Requirements), but under some conditions chapters 5, 6, 7, 8, 12 and 13 may also apply.

Chapter 2, Fundamental Requirements, requires an adequate number of safe, well-marked exits based on the number of occupants and the occupancy hazard presented. Chapter 5, Means of Egress; 6, Features of Fire Protection; and 7, Building Service Equipment, set forth methods of meeting the requirements of chapter 2. In addition, chapter 8, Places of Assembly, and chapter 12, Mercantile Occupancies, may be applicable to either the entire building or a portion thereof.

Protection of Historic Buildings

Since every building presents unique problems, any attempt to set forth specific requirements would be futile. However, some general comments regarding historic buildings and their protection are appropriate.

Historic buildings represent an inheritance for future generations. One of the objectives of preserving such buildings is to preserve the original structure as an alternative to a replication. In addition, the building should be seen by the public. Finally, safety must be provided. The restoration and showing of such buildings is much easier to accomplish than providing safety. Safety is a problem when the occupancy has changed. Many buildings, once used as single-family residences, become places of assembly because of the number of persons who tour the buildings at one time. The provision of sufficient exits alone can at times present what seem to be insurmountable obstacles; swinging doors out that originally swung in, providing either larger or additional doors to satisfy requirements for exit capacity and marking the exits and routes of exit travel. In addition, there are flame-spread requirements for interior surface finishes and decorations that limit the speed at which flames can spread along the surface of a material.

Possible Solutions

In most cases the person responsible for enforcing a code has some discretionary powers. In exercising these powers this official will usually want to be certain that the intent of the code is being met.

One method of providing the code official with considerable latitude in which to exercise discretionary powers is through automatic extinguishing systems. These may be in the form of automatic sprinkler systems, high expansion foam systems, Halon systems and carbon dioxide systems. There are six major types of automatic sprinkler system. One that lends itself well to historic buildings is the pre-action system. This system has piping and heads like any other automatic sprinkler system, but there is air, under 8–10 ounces of pressure, in all of the piping on the building side of the main control valve. There is also a network of heat sensing devices throughout the building. When these devices detect heat, they activate a solenoid that opens the main valve and allows water to flow into the piping. Still, no water is released into the building until the sprinkler head becomes hot enough to release and allow the head to discharge water onto the fire.

Other possible solutions are to limit or control the amount of combustible material to be introduced in the building; the use of early warning devices, such as smoke detectors, heat detectors or a combination of both; and employee training.

Historic buildings can be restored so as to provide safety to the structure and occupants. It may require imagination to conceal some of the safeguards from view. At times they may not be concealable at all. However, it is better to allow some safeguards to be seen, ensuring the safety of the building and occupants, than to omit them in dogmatically following the theme of authenticity, and lose forever a cherished part of the past and take a chance with human life.

Fire Safety and Historic Preservation in Federally Owned Buildings

KAREL H. YASKO, FAIA

Karel H. Yasko, FAIA, is counsellor to the administrator for Fine Arts and Historic Preservation in the U.S. General Services Administration. Formerly state architect for Wisconsin, he was involved in the state building code, especially as it related to fire safety and experimental contemporary architecture.

If the title "Preservation and Building Codes" had been strictly applied, the General Services Administration would have had little place on the program, except to talk enthusiastically about historic preservation. While GSA designs and constructs government buildings on a large scale and maintains a broad historic preservation program, it does not write or publish any building codes; there is no federal building code. By right of sovereign domain, GSA as a federal agency is legally exempt from building codes instituted by state or local governments. As part of the federal government GSA is self-insured and thus is not subject to the fire insurance provisions so strongly apparent in building codes.

This position does not mean that the GSA does not abide by the intent of building codes; on the contrary, many GSA fire safety innovations have brought about changes in state and local codes. Through size alone —10,000 federally owned and leased buildings, 1,700 ongoing construction projects and a $1 billion construction budget—GSA exercises a major impact on building codes nationwide. Exemption from local codes also places on GSA a moral and legislative responsibility to the persons who use GSA buildings and to the direct business of the federal agencies that use GSA facilities and services.

Commitment to Safety and Preservation

GSA has a dual commitment to safety and to historic preservation. It is committed to the objectives of both the National Historic Preservation Act of 1966 and Executive Order 11593 on the historic preservation of buildings. In addition, GSA is fully committed to provide, throughout its facilities, levels of safety that protect from accident, fire or other harm employees, visitors and any others who enter these buildings. Such levels equal or exceed the intent of the

Occupational Safety and Health Act, P.L. 91-596, and Executive Order 11807 on federal programs relating to the act.

GSA believes its policies create a balance between society's need to preserve its heritage and societal concern with individual safety. To strike such a balance is not an easy matter in the face of the classic problem of the good of the whole versus the rights of the individual. While much flexibility is possible, a hard core of protection remains that cannot be cracked, so GSA resorts to compromise through maximum innovation, using a systems concept rather than hard and fast specific requirements. Based on an overall level of safety needs, this goal-oriented system permits simultaneous consideration of life protection and the protection of property.

Analyzing Fire Potential

The primary objective, then, is to determine the overall safety level GSA wishes to establish. Against this level GSA analyzes the fire potential, which is the probable size and intensity of the fire and its products as well as the resultant risk to human life. Analysis must break down the elements of fire potential: fire energy, confinement and suppression.

Fire energy begins with the fuel and the surrounding conditions controlling or supporting the way it burns and how it spreads. Paper or wood can be fuel considerations, while floor plans and ventilation as well as wood finishes, such as paint and varnish, affect the control or support of the fire and influence its spread. If these fuel sources occur in all areas surrounding the original fire point, the spread can become a point-to-point race between the fire and the feeder sources.

The next task is to confine the size and extent of the fire to as small an area as possible. Compartmentalization (better known as the floor plan) and the capabilities of the building's structural system are primary considerations; in historic buildings both are critical and common problems. The plan layouts of some of the buildings allow easy confinement of fire, except in open stairways. To enclose these stairways negates much of their design quality. Control doors in the corridors before the stairways are one effective safety solution. The framing system is perhaps more of a problem in many older structures. Wood joists are common, as are certain types of brick arch construction that can be susceptible to failure. Cast-iron columns provide a false sense of security; their failure in fire can collapse the framing system, destroying the basic architectural and structural integrity of the building.

Methods of renovation and restoration work can either improve the situation or increase the fire risk. Since one objective in historic preservation is preservation of as much of the structure's essential quality as possible while creating protection against fire, GSA focuses on the ability to extinguish the fire at its point of origin. An encompassing word is "suppression."

Manual and automatic extinguishing mechanisms are first considerations for suppression. These include a review of the capabilities of the responding fire department, fire detection systems and, most importantly, automatic fire extinguishing systems. Philosophically, GSA seeks a suppression device that controls the fire with minimum intrusion on the historic character of the building.

The automatic sprinkler system is effective because it can reduce the amount of rearrangement that might be necessary otherwise, and it need not detract from the appearance of the building. Sprinklers can protect a building that might otherwise be unsafe or unsuitable without major renovations.

An automatic sprinkler system is not necessarily the solution a designer picks readily. Often it is rejected off-hand while expensive and extreme solutions are pursued to the detriment of the preservation objective. GSA recommends a second look at the situation and the problem.

In his other efforts to establish the overall level of safety the designer may encounter some existing building conditions that are minor in the total, but do present tolerable risks. Recommendations may be made by the designer to forego the expensive and complicated solution and accept the risks. Such risks can be tolerated under the condition that necessary safeguards for protection of human life are provided and that the risks are clearly understood and will be tolerated by all concerned, particularly the occupants.

Protecting Human Life

GSA believes people are the measure in fire safety of building construction. It is natural, therefore, that surrounding the fire potential (which is at the core of the problem) as a reactive force is the protection of human life. GSA has divided consideration of human safety into four elements of the system, with appropriate labels: life-support, people-movement, emergency communication and emergency preparedness. All are closely related without priority.

In the life-support element GSA is concerned with providing a building environment where a person can survive tolerably from the moment of fire ignition until free and clear of the building. When the structure is small and the building population low, it may be necessary to maintain only a stairway and exit path free and clear of smoke and toxic fumes. In larger, taller buildings with higher population densities, especially where visitors are unfamiliar with the structure, the problem becomes critical. Since federal buildings in the GSA historic preservation program are rarely more than three or four stories high, GSA has not had to be overly concerned with life support.

People-movement concerns itself primarily with vertical and horizontal circulation: stairs, exits and corridors. In many GSA historical buildings these items, especially stairways, present serious problems. To solve them GSA attempts to develop alternate mechanisms that will provide two alternate routes of egress for any person in the building. Either route must provide access to a safeguarded point on the person's floor level where access to the outside is possible without having to reenter any area potentially involved in fire. The shorter of these routes should be similar to standard stairwell arrangements and available within 90 seconds after a person begins an exit pattern.

Because fire safety solutions may vary according to the individual character of the historic preservation project and as a result may require unfamiliar exit patterns, emergency communication systems may have to be developed. In some instances, in case of fire, coded alarms based on previously issued instructions would go to each building occupant. For other situations, with perhaps more complex conditions, the alarm message would go only to a cadre of selected persons trained to guide occupants and visitors to safety. The selection of the final emergency communication system should depend primarily on the size of the building, its use and its plan arrangement.

Emergency preparedness, an aspect of all parts of the GSA system, forms its unifying element. It indicates the extent to which the designer has determined the individual character of the building, its occupants and the capabilities of its operators.

The GSA system approach to fire safety in historic preservation projects does not provide the designer with a permit to ignore building codes. Instead the designer must pursue a cautious and imaginative path to provide a high level of safety that allows for maximum innovation. GSA expects a mechanism that can provide an optimal solution to the common problem of preservation versus safety of the individual.

Occupational Safety and Health Administration Interest in Building Requirements for Historic Buildings

THOMAS H. SEYMOUR

Thomas H. Seymour has been technical assistant to the director of the Office of Standards, U.S. Department of Labor, since the beginning of the Occupational Safety and Health Administration.

The Occupational Safety and Health Administration (OSHA) was created by the Occupational Safety and Health Act of 1970 (OSH Act). The act authorizes OSHA to develop, promulgate and enforce occupational safety and health standards for every place in the United States employing one or more persons.

OSHA is concerned with employers and employees only and is not charged with responsibility or authority over the safety and health of the general public. Furthermore, employers are responsible for their employees only.

There are exceptions to coverage under the OSH Act. OSHA has no direct authority over any federal employer. The federal agency executive is responsible for an occupational safety and health program for agency employees and must develop standards that are consistent with OSHA standards. State and local government employees are not covered by federal OSHA authority, but they can be covered by state authority if the state has an agreement with OSHA. Employers and employees covered by other federal laws that contain occupational safety and health coverage are exempt from coverage by the OSH Act if regulations have been issued. Also, OSHA does not cover employees while performing ordinary domestic tasks in private residences and the clergy and other employees while participating in religious services.

OSHA coverage of historic sites and buildings that house historical displays raises more questions than answers. OSHA must find answers to these questions, in particular: How many buildings, landmarks or displays are deemed to have historical value? Is the National Register the only list of historic sites of concern to OSHA or are the state and charitable organization lists of historic buildings deemed to have historical value also of concern to OSHA? How many employees are involved in operating and maintaining these historic buildings? What hazards are faced by persons employed in historic buildings? Is the entire building designated as a landmark or only a portion of the building or site?

Because of Executive Order 11593 and its purposes, OSHA recognizes that historic sites present special problems and wishes to cooperate with the Advisory Council on Historic Preservation and other interested organizations.

Any employer whose employees work in historic buildings and who believes it impossible to meet the exact requirements of OSHA standards may apply for a variance. The application for variance must show that the proposed alternate methods or procedures provide as safe and healthful a workplace as would exist with compliance with OSHA standards.

Certain OSHA standards do directly affect building code and model code requirements. OSHA has promulgated electrical wiring standards, plumbing and sanitation standards, life safety or exit standards, special local ventilation or exhaust ventilation standards and standards in certain other areas as well. As an example, a historic building that has no indoor toilet facilities is not necessarily in violation of OSHA plumbing and sanitation standards. The employer can provide toilet facilities for employees in another building on the site or adjacent to the site with the proper number of toilets and lavatories as prescribed by OSHA standards. OSHA has not prescribed any travel distance to such toilet facilities.

OSHA recognizes that historic buildings present special problems for its occupational safety and health program. OSHA has met and corresponded with the staff of the Advisory Council on Historic Preservation and with other interested parties over mutual concerns. OSHA desires guidance on how to regulate historic landmarks and what options are available; a number of questions are confronting OSHA and it is seeking answers. As of this time, OSHA has issued no policy statement regarding historic landmarks and looks forward to resolving these questions through cooperative efforts with the Advisory Council on Historic Preservation and other interested organizations.

Old Buildings and the National Conference of States on Building Codes and Standards

BERNARD E. CABELUS

Bernard E. Cabelus is Connecticut state building inspector and immediate past chairman of the National Conference of States on Building Codes and Standards.

The National Conference of States on Building Codes and Standards (NCSBCS) is an organization composed of one governor's delegate from each of the 50 states and three territories. The conference has worked for the uniformity of building codes and regulations throughout the nation and supports national consensus on standards. It encourages those working for reciprocity between states so that buildings and building components can be shipped both within and between states. At the present time, the same mobile home regulations apply in about 45 states, a figure undreamed of 10 years ago.

It is increasingly evident that many persons involved in the preservation and utilization of historic buildings have a lack of understanding of building codes, fire codes and all of the various regulatory areas that govern the construction, use and occupancy of buildings. An understanding of these areas is vital. When looking at a patient, a doctor must analyze all of the bodily functions prior to proceeding on a course of action leading to the proper treatment and cure.

For a long time an acute need has existed for persons interested in the restoration of historic buildings to meet with persons in charge of promulgating building regulations in the various states and municipalities of this nation. Persons involved in the regulation of buildings and structures are increasingly dismayed at the quantity of state and local legislation that proposes to eradicate all building code provisions for historic buildings. It is time, therefore, for those concerned for the preservation of true American history and those involved in the administration of public safety to sit down and work together in order to establish a standard for historic buildings that can be incorporated into the building codes of this nation.

The State of Connecticut has established historic districts such as Mystic Seaport, which is a restoration of a seaport dating from the time when whaling was at its height in this country. The town of Wethersfield, which claims—along with Hartford and Windsor—to be the first settlement in the state of Connecticut, dating from 1633, has established a historic district that, in the author's opinion, is second to none. Many other cities and towns are following this example, the town of Berlin being the most recent to pass legislation creating a historic district. This town has many buildings that are over 200 years old.

Unfortunately, persons interested in the "fast dollar," and in evading building regulations have taken the opportunity of being acclaimed as those most interested in the restoration of old buildings. For example, a Connecticut restaurant owner tried every possible way to move a dilapidated colonial building into the fire districts of a city under the guise that it was a historic building. Fire districts are established in densely built up areas, where a more restrictive type of construction is employed to avoid conflagrations. He wanted all the safety rules waived, including those that would protect the people of the city and any other person who visited the building. His plan was to completely gut the structure, leaving only the exterior shell, and to install a bar and a restaurant that would seat about 225 persons. This plan would have made the building a place of public assembly under Connecticut law. The building, in the author's opinion, would have had no historical significance whatsoever because of the extensive alteration.

Historical societies serve a much-needed purpose in determining what is or is not historic, and if they approach a situation wisely, there is no question that historical societies will receive cooperation from the building authorities. Bills have been submitted to legislators that would have wiped out every building code provision as not applicable to historic buildings; the building official would have been deprived of the right to inspect for structural safety, wiring, heating, plumbing or any other component of the building or structure, even though the building existed in an extremely dangerous and/or hazardous condition. Legislators have been besieged by historical groups wishing to have an old building torn down and moved 10 towns away to be re-erected for resale as a residence. They have specifically requested that the state legislature waive all requirements of inspection, regardless of the building's structural strength or existing hazardous conditions, all because the building was aged. In one instance, the developer who was to move the building complained strongly because the building official was requiring him to furnish necessary information for an evaluation of possible building hazards.

It should be obvious to all that the cabin where Abe Lincoln lived as a boy and the home that Jesse and Frank James lived in certainly played parts in American history. These and similar buildings should be preserved and maintained in their original condition if at all possible. However, I do not agree with persons who say that every building 100 years old or older is a historic building. In making an unofficial survey of a Connecticut town with a population of 35,000, I found that more than 600 buildings could be classified as historic using age as a guideline. Six hundred buildings free of safety regulations would create a serious hazard and threaten human life.

It is time for persons involved in the preservation of historic buildings to sit down with building officials, fire officials, design professionals and all others vitally interested in buildings and their construction and preservation. It will only be by open communication among historians, code officials and design professionals that a consensus can be developed as to what can and should be incorporated in the nation's major building codes. The time for procrastination is past; if this problem is to be attacked and resolved, action must be prompt. I shall formally propose to the National Conference of States on Building Codes and Standards that they become actively engaged in supporting and working toward the establishment of a workable solution through a safe consensus standard that will both regulate and allow for restoration of historic buildings in the United States.

Until such time as a national consensus standard can be developed, the problem of historic buildings will be like driftwood at sea—drifting with the tide. Virginia will take a step, another state will take the next step and New Orleans will take another. When this happens, a design professional from one area will not be able to take a contract or a job for restoration elsewhere because the requirements will be different—and this country will again have a system of highly localized building codes. This subject of historic buildings is as complicated for architects and preservationists as the dilemma for building officials is when applying the safe exit and panic hardware provisions of the building code to a state prison—and that is a problem. Milton Grigg of Virginia has given strong support for state building codes. The National Conference of States on Building Codes and Standards has developed a Model State Building Code Act, which has been accepted by the Council of State Governments. The code was distributed to all state legislatures and is available without charge from Francis Ventre, Secretariat of the NCSBCS, National Bureau of Standards, Center for Building Technology, Washington, D.C. 20234.

Connecticut was the first state to have a complete statewide mandatory building code that covered all types of construction. The Connecticut state law also requires certification of all building officials and assistant building officials through the office of the state building inspector.

Connecticut has for the last five years been conducting continuing education courses and may have an associate degree program in building code administration commencing in fall 1974 at the state technical colleges. This program will be a major breakthrough in professionalizing the building official. Building officials, like design professionals, vary in competence; therefore, Connecticut law has provided for both educational programs and appeals by aggrieved persons both on the local and state levels.

Building officials are a bit different from the fire officials. The fire people put fires out. Building officials try to anticipate and regulate buildings—to design them so people can get out when there are fires. Exits are most important. Early warning devices such as sprinklers do save property; I am not going to say they save lives—I have a big question on that.

The 50 state industrial advisers, with the National Bureau of Standards serving as their secretariat, have shown how state, private and federal agencies can work together for the betterment of all. The support and encouragement that Richard Roberts, director of the National Bureau of Standards, and his staff gave the NCSBCS is most appreciated. Thomas Seymour of OSHA has provided excellent liaison to the Conference of States since 1972. HUD has also been working with the National Conference, and its attorneys, headed by Arthur Newburg, have been assisting the National Conference with legal work. This type of cooperation among state government, federal government and the private sector should continue because it shows the rest of the country that state lines are imaginary lines and that our problems in Connecticut are the problems of Mississippi, Texas or California.

Special Liability and Insurance Problems of Historic Buildings

JOHN A. WADLEWSKI

John A. Wadlewski is assistant to the vice president, Casualty Division, Insurance Services Office.

When an insurance contract is negotiated, the insured sets in motion an army of people and a battery of services geared to fulfillment of the contract for the benefit of the insured.

Each of the skilled professionals involved with insurance—lawyers, claims adjusters, actuaries, forms writers and others—deserves a job description detailing how he or she benefits the insured. Lack of space precludes this approach and so, with apologies to all these professionals, the following is a description of the work of only one insurance professional, the insurance underwriter, and a look at a historic building through this insurance professional's eyes.

An insurance underwriter is better described than defined. The insured, usually through an insurance agent, requires and seeks insurance coverage for possible liability exposures. The insurance company wants to provide the coverage, but since it is not a charitable institution it also wants to make a profit. The insured and the insurance company may have their own attorneys, safety engineers, managers, agents and safety teams, all with an interest in the contract and all with recommendations to be entered in the negotiations. It is the job of the professional underwriter to coordinate these varied interests into a final product not only acceptable by all but with each party feeling justified in the acceptance.

The information about the insured comes from a written application. The application is unfortunately lacking in detailed information but provides enough for the underwriter to begin work.

Naming the Insured

The name of the applicant is probably the first detail the underwriter notes. The name to be put on the policy as "named insured" must actually be that of the legal entity that is to be covered. The underwriter will not issue a policy in the name of "Jones House 1817" unless that is the legal name. In most instances a name such as Jones House 1817 identifies the exposure but does not identify the legal owner.

The owner and operator of the Jones House is probably a historical society, and it is this society that must be identified—as the Chester Historical Society, Inc., for example.

When the owner is properly named, the officers of the association are automatically covered while acting in that capacity. An endorsement added to the policy may provide coverage for all members of the historical association named, with respect to their liability for activities of the association or for activities performed on behalf of the association other than practice or participation in any game or sport.

Determining Liability Exposures

Having clarified who is covered, the underwriter then focuses on what is to be covered. It is assumed here that the insured wants all owner liabilities covered and that the basic liability policy for a historic building has been purchased. It is now the underwriter's task to help discover exposures that may not be covered by the basic policy.

If a historic building is purchased by a historical association, often extensive renovations must be made Purchase and renovation require funds. Fundraising events—dances, exhibitions, fairs and parties —must therefore be sponsored; these events can create liabilities that may be covered by insurance.

A historical association, the named insured, is composed of persons who periodically hold business meetings. The meeting rooms may be owned by the association or they may be rented or donated for meetings. The historical association is responsible for the safety of the public at these meetings, and it needs protection for liability accruing from the meetings.

It is not unusual, in fact it is usual, that when meeting rooms and halls are rented for meetings and fundraising events the lessor will require a contract containing a hold-harmless clause; that is, the lessee will under contract assume the lessor's liability. The degree of assumption of such liability varies with each contract, and even if the contract is covered by contractual insurance the scope of the contract itself may be broader than the scope of the contractual policy covering the assumed liability. Legal counsel should be obtained before any contract is signed.

Eventually, a historical association may raise enough money to purchase the building. However, the owner may sell the building only and not the land, so the building must be moved to another site. Moving buildings is a hazardous undertaking. Damage to the building itself is not a consideration for the liability underwriter, but damages and liabilities that result from moving the building are. Electrical wiring and gas piping must be disconnected, the building must be elevated onto wheels for transport and then it must be transported through traffic to its new location. Each of these activities constitutes a hazard of concern to the underwriter.

Because the historical association initiates all moving activities that can cause injury, it can ultimately be held liable even though it is not doing any of the work. *American Jurisprudence*, vol. 13, states, "If the fall of a building in the course of construction is the result of a violation of law committed by contractor, and the owner knows of such violation and sanctions it, he may be held responsible, but only where the violation is the proximate cause of the injury."

The association can protect itself by hiring a licensed contractor of good repute so that the association cannot be accused of carelessly hiring incompetents, by requesting a hold-harmless contract from the contractor-mover, by being added onto the contractor's policy as an additional insured and by insuring itself for contingent liability coverage.

In several states there are "safe place to work" laws which require an owner, such as a historical association, to provide a safe place to work, even though the persons working and thus exposed to injury are the employees of a contractor or subcontractor. While workmen's compensation insurance protects the employer in accordance with state law, the association has no such protection and can be sued for an unlimited amount and must protect itself.

Finally, an association may open a building to the public. Employees or volunteers throughout the building help make the public comfortable and safe. If these employees are salaried it is safe to say that in most states an association, as an employer, must provide workmen's compensation insurance coverage for its employees. For nonsalaried, volunteer workers a historical association may provide voluntary workmen's compensation coverage and should purchase employers liability insurance to protect itself.

Voluntary workmen's compensation, as its name implies, refers to an employer's act of purchasing insurance providing statutory compensation benefits to those employees for whom statutory compensation is not required. Where workmen's compensation is by legal mandate, workmen's compensation is the sole recourse of an employee against an employer for reimbursement of injuries. There are no such restrictions for voluntary compensation; the injured employee can either collect voluntary workmen's compensation benefits or sue the employer for liability. The insured is protected for employee suits by purchasing employers liability insurance.

The Comprehensive General Liability policy is the basic insurance policy being sold or purchased these days. This policy incorporates many separate liability insurance policies (Manufacturers and Contractors; Owners, Landlords and Tenants; Owners and Contractors Protective, etc.) into one document that provides the insured with coverage for all basic liability exposures. The Comprehensive General Liability policy is mentioned here to emphasize the point that this type of policy will automatically cover a multiplicity of exposures. For example, the insured may insure one building and forget another or purchase a building later; the policy will provide coverage for all.

With this comprehensive coverage in mind, the underwriter must make sure that all of the exposures of the insured have been considered, not just those of which the underwriter is advised. To collect a proper premium and to establish a meaningful safety program, the entire risk must be considered.

A historic building may be part of a group of buildings. Speedwell Village in Morristown, N.J., is an example of an *entire* complex that must be considered for insurance engineering and for insurance coverage. Liability exposures may include parking lots, picnic areas, playgrounds, walkways, hiking paths, refreshment and souvenir stands, campgrounds and parks. Some historical areas may have train rides, animal rides, museums, theaters and even zoos.

Another hazard must be considered; the underwriter calls it "personal injury." When numbers of people gather, many of them will be children. This is especially true of historic sites. Where there are children, the lack of restraint on some children is likely to result in running, chasing, hiding and climbing into forbidden places. Consequently, it is necessary at times for employees of the insured to apply physical restraints to these visitors. No one can predict when some parent will feel that a child has been restrained too severely or unjustly and will sue.

A typical endorsement providing personal injury coverage includes these injuries: "(a) false arrest, detention or imprisonment, or malicious prosecution; (b) the publication or utterance of a libel or slander or of other defamatory or disparaging material, or a publication or utterance in violation of an individual's right of privacy; except publications or utterances in the course of or related to advertising, broadcasting or telecasting activities conducted by or on behalf of the named insured; (c) wrongful entry or eviction or other invasion of the right of private occupancy."

Some of these exposures may appear farfetched, but these types of exposures are a potential liability for the organization. The association seems to have a moral and social responsibility to protect the public by purchasing insurance coverage for these potential hazards.

Determining Physical Hazards

If, rather than looking at the entire risk, the underwriter concentrates on the structure itself, serious consideration must be given to the physical condition of the building in determining whether it will be safe for its proposed use. Since these are observable physical characteristics, the insurance application does not contain this information, and the underwriter requests an engineering report. The engineering report is a concise description of the building, a list and description of physical hazards and a recommendation of how to mitigate the risk if possible.

The safety engineer examines paths leading to and around the building, noting structural deficiencies such as potholes, crumbled cement, cracks and general unevenness. The windows and window ledges are examined for flowerpots that might fall and for loose window screens and shutters. The safety engineer comments on the condition of the stairs and its risers, noting any loose or broken boards. Does the door open properly? Can a young, crippled or aged person get trapped behind doors in case of fire? All floors are examined for flowerpots that might fall and for loose Wall hangings may be loose, electric switches exposed or light fixtures in danger of falling. A stairway may be worn and narrow and handrails may be missing. The lighting may be too dim or may blind the visitor at a crucial step or landing on the stairway. Everything is checked.

Once the inspection is completed, recommendations are made to improve existing conditions. Recommendations may be to nail down a loose board, put up a sign warning of a low doorway and hire more personnel to supervise and control visitors. The recommendation list is long enough to make the risk acceptable from a safety standpoint. This particular historic building has now met all the standards of safety except that the main stairway, trod by figures of history, is worn and potentially a dangerous tripping hazard. Because it is the original stairway and because it has historical value, replacing or changing the stairway in any way would be unacceptable to the preservationist. In such circumstances, even the cold heart of the underwriter will find it impossible to demand a change.

If someone is injured because of the worn stairs and proceeds to sue for damages, it is the belief of one experienced claims adjuster and attorney that a majority court opinion holds that "reasonableness" on the part of the insured would be a factor in determining fault. In other words, the worn stairs *per se* would not constitute fault on the part of the insured, and the claim would be settled on the basis of whether or not the insured used reasonable precautions to prevent accidents. If the stairs are so worn that any use would be dangerous, there is no doubt that the average underwriter will not insure the risk unless the stairway in question is roped off from use. In other words, the reasonable action is to prevent the use of such hazards rather than to depend on the visitor's assuming the risk.

The underwriter is careful to obtain as complete a knowledge as possible of the physical hazards of the risk. Persons on holiday may relax to a point of carelessness, and the underwriter must make sure that, despite themselves, they will not be injured.

Determining the Premium

Perhaps a word about the premium is in order. The underwriter has gathered all the necessary information about a risk and decides to cover the insured, believing that the insurance company can accept the risk and make some profit doing it. A general liability policy will be written providing premises liability coverage. The premises liability will cover injuries arising out of the grounds and the building. Endorsed, the policy can cover the various contractual obligations previously mentioned, as well as personal injury. The voluntary workmen's compensation and the employer's liability have enough of their own specific provisions to require a separate workmen's compensation policy. The automobile liability exposures have not been mentioned but automobiles owned by the insured represent a liability exposure. Liabilities from individually owned automobiles driven on behalf of the insured are not as obvious. An automobile policy is needed, of course. When all of these needs have been decided, the policy is "rated" to determine the premium.

One of the functions of insurance is to distribute the risk or loss of a few among the many. The most equitable method is to identify risks by class and to collect enough money from that class to pay the losses of the class. In this way all hotels are in the "hotels" class, all churches in the "church" class, etc. To make this system work, the class must be large enough to make available data credible. Of course, more data results in a more credible class rate. Unfortunately, historic buildings are not numerous enough to constitute a class. The underwriter must rate them in accordance with some credible class that has similar liability exposures. There are several classes that have similar exposures: for example, museums, model homes, halls and exhibition buildings. With such a choice, there is little doubt that in the hands of a professional underwriter the final rate will be adequate for the risk.

Summary

In looking at a risk, the underwriter examines the application, checks the "named insured," checks the liability exposures and then asks for an engineering report of the risk, makes sure the proper policies are issued and checks that these policies are properly endorsed and rated. In short, the underwriter has taken care of the historical association insurance needs for coverage, the insurance company needs in making the risk as safe as possible and in collecting the proper premium and, finally, the public by giving them a safe place to visit.

Future Action

Future Directions for the Occupational Safety and Health Administration and Historic Preservation

JOHN M. FOWLER

John M. Fowler is associate legal counsel with the Advisory Council on Historic Preservation.

In order to explain the role of the Advisory Council on Historic Preservation in future actions concerning building codes and historic preservation, it is necessary to explore the present role of the council in this area. As adviser to the President and to Congress on matters of historic preservation, the Advisory Council has a primary responsibility to coordinate the activities of the federal government and its constituent agencies as they relate to the preservation of the nation's cultural resources. It was in this capacity that the council confronted the problem of building codes and preservation in the Occupational Safety and Health Act of 1970.

In early 1972, the potential impact of the Occupational Safety and Health Administration (OSHA) on historic resources was brought to council attention by the owners of several historic properties faced with OSHA compliance. The scope of this impact soon became evident. As Thomas H. Seymour of the Department of Labor has noted (see "OSHA Interest in Building Requirements," p. 79), the act is all-inclusive, covering virtually all places where persons work for employers. This means that a broad range of historic properties, beyond those classifiable as commercial or industrial, are affected by OSHA. Buildings being restored as museums or rehabilitated for adaptive use will come under OSHA purview if they become places of employment, and once a building is within the scope of OSHA all applicable standards must be met. Faced with this extensive and potentially severe threat to national historic preservation policies, the Advisory Council informed the Department of Labor of the extent of this problem and sought a means of solving it so that the independent objectives of both occupational health and safety and historic preservation could be achieved. With the assistance of the National Trust for Historic Preservation, the National Park Service and the Smithsonian Institution, the Advisory Council and the Department of Labor studied the conflicts between OSHA and preservation objectives and identified the areas in which some accommodation of these objectives could be reached.

Defining the Problem

Initial discussions with the Department of Labor confirmed the extent of the problem. Any employer with at least one employee must comply with OSHA standards, regardless of whether the employer is engaged in a profit-making operation. Beyond businesses, which clearly fell within OSHA, it became apparent that many nonprofit museums and foundation-owned buildings would be required to meet OSHA standards. As if the breadth of kinds of operations covered was not enough, the council soon learned that OSHA permitted states to implement their own safety and health plans instead of federal standards. The prospect of 50 separate state programs under OSHA would substantially complicate matters compared with a single federal agency administering the act. Finally, initial consultations with OSHA representatives revealed the limited latitude for administrative discretion at the federal and state level under the Occupational Safety and Health Act and the consequently narrow range of possible solutions to the problem.

Faced with this somewhat discouraging situation, the council, along with its National Trust and National Park Service allies, sought to identify the areas that required action. An initial step was the definition of which historic properties would qualify for any special treatment that might be forthcoming under OSHA. There was also the essential question of what modifications were possible in the OSHA process to accommodate historic preservation objectives. Should a solution be worked out with the federal standards, there remained the question of similar recognition of preservation in the numerous state plans to be submitted for federal approval, replacing federally enforced OSHA standards. Within these three major areas, the council and the Department of Labor searched for solutions.

Identifying Historic Properties

Drawing on the expertise of the National Park Service, the council approached the problem of identifying historic properties for OSHA exemption purposes. Because OSHA standards are federally established and enforced, it was decided that the basic federal inventory of historic properties, the National Register of Historic Places, would be used as the index of recognized historical significance for OSHA. The National Park Service agreed to attempt to identify those aspects of a historic property that might be affected by the application of OSHA standards, making it then possible to separate nonhistoric features that could be modified to meet OSHA standards from those whose modification for OSHA compliance would impair the historic integrity of the resource. This distinction between historic and nonhistoric features is one of the central elements in the solution arrived at by the Advisory Council and the Department of Labor.

Modifying the OSHA Process

With the general framework of the identification process established, the council staff met with OSHA representatives to explore means of considering the value of the historic resources in the OSHA process. Initial attempts to obtain a blanket exemption or variance from all applicable OSHA standards for any properly recognized historic property proved fruitless because of restrictions inherent in the OSHA statute itself. However, the attempt pointed the way to what is hoped will provide a satisfactory solution in most cases.

Under OSHA, any employer may apply for a variance from a particular standard on the grounds that present working conditions are as safe as conditions where the standard technically is applied. While this remedy is open to any employer, whether located in a historic building or not, it is a complex and arduous process. To alleviate this stumbling block, the Department of Labor has indicated a willingness to make the process of obtaining such a variance easier when historic buildings are involved. Initially, the Department of Labor proposes to adopt a policy recognizing the need to accommodate both the preservation of historic buildings and the goals of occupational safety and health. This policy will direct OSHA officials, when considering variances for historic properties, to give maximum consideration to innovative alternatives that meet preservation and OSHA goals.

To further smooth the path to a historic preservation variance, the Department of Labor has suggested that modifications in the normal inspection process might be made to facilitate the identification of problem areas in a historic property and to assist the owner in presenting a justification for variance.

Recognizing Preservation in the State Plans

While this approach seems suitable for federal implementation of OSHA standards, the state plans required further attention. State plans require approval by federal OSHA officials, providing federal officials with an opportunity to insure that federal policy toward historic buildings is reflected in state plans. One further means of exercising federal control over state plans lies in the general responsibility of the state to conduct its plan in a manner consistent with established federal OSHA policies, including those for historic properties. In this way some degree of federal guidance can be exercised over state action to allow the same kind of treatment for historic properties as is incorporated in the federal OSHA program.

The substance of the OSHA historic preservation proposal has been agreed on and action is now required to implement the plan. After the proposal is implemented, the Advisory Council will gather information on its success in meeting the problem as initially identified. Individual professional experience with particular preservation projects will be essential for accurate feedback, and the Advisory Council would appreciate information on these experiences with OSHA as restoration and adaptive use projects are undertaken. On the basis of this proposal's success, or lack of it, in accommodating preservation and occupational safety and health, the council will be able to determine what future steps are necessary. Failure of the process now being worked out by the Advisory Council and the Department of Labor may prompt the council to recommend to Congress that a statutory amendment to the Occupational Safety and Health Act is the only way to achieve the objectives of the national historic preservation policy in the face of OSHA. Should this course of action be followed, it will require the active support of the entire preservation community, especially of those who confront the problems of OSHA in their professional lives. The Advisory Council hopes they will be there to meet the challenge.

Future Action of the American Institute of Architects

WILLIAM BODLEY LANE, AIA

William B. Lane, AIA, is a practicing architect in St. Louis, Mo. He is chairman of the AIA Committee on Historic Resources.

In considering appropriate action for a particular organization to take on a subject, in this case preservation and building codes, it is important to properly assess the nature, abilities and structure of that organization.

Certainly the National Trust for Historic Preservation proved its effectiveness in sponsoring this conference, as evidenced by the many excellent papers that provide an opportunity to better understand the viewpoints of the several interested groups, organizations and agencies.

Committee on Historic Resources

The American Institute of Architects (AIA) Committee on Historic Resources will review the many ideas expressed at the conference, study more deeply some of the suggestions and then make definite recommendations to the AIA board of directors. Since the AIA is composed of licensed professional artists, the problem of balancing aesthetic and public safety considerations is not new to its members. Confidence that the Committee on Historic Resources will produce workable suggestions is understandable when one considers that the committee includes such persons as Orin Bullock, Giorgio Cavaglieri, Milton Grigg, Nicholas Holmes and Russell Keune. The consulting members include Karel Yasko and James Massey.

Methods of Implementation

Once the policy is established, the AIA has a variety of organizational channels through which to influence the thinking of architects, preservationists, government officials and local building code officials. As an adjunct to the Committee on Historic Resources, the AIA has a nationwide network of state preservation coordinators. These architects are expected to keep in touch with preservation-minded architects, individuals, organizations and code officials in their states. The AIA also has a fulltime Director of Codes and Regulations, currently James R. Dowling, who advises AIA members and will continue to help on these matters. A national AIA Committee on Building Codes and a Commission on Government Affairs will also play a part in AIA activities.

As things are progressing now, it is a matter of convincing the various building codes organizations to include a section that gives discretionary powers to building officials when historic buildings are considered. The next step is to work on the local level to insure that these sections remain in the local codes and are used properly. All concerned must be encouraged to seek alternate solutions that give equal protection to the buildings and to the people if at all possible. This process is the way the American Institute of Architects expects to help carry out the purpose of the Preservation and Building Codes conference.

Background

It was routine AIA staff questions about possible problems with historic preservation and professional liability for the safety of a building that first led to consideration of code exceptions in May 1971 by the Committee on Historic Resources. Henry Chambers investigated professional liability insurance. The author initiated preliminary discussions with Fred B. Meckfessel, Jr., a St. Louis building commissioner active in the national organization of the Building Officials and Code Administrators. By December 1971 Nicholas Holmes was interested in the problem, after some negative code experiences in Alabama. In July 1972 Giorgio Cavaglieri wrote a provocative letter on the subject to Holmes, who began pressuring the AIA staff. The staff put Holmes in touch with Murvan Maxwell and his reply convinced the committee that he was knowledgeable on code and preservation matters. This previous involvement partially explains why it is such a pleasure to attend this conference when both BOCA and the Southern Building Code Congress are considering special provisions for historic preservation.

Future Plans of the National Trust for Historic Preservation

RUSSELL V. KEUNE, AIA

Russell V. Keune, AIA, is director of the Department of Field Services, National Trust for Historic Preservation.

National Trust plans for the future relative to building codes are best expressed by comments on the areas in which the Trust operates at present. The first of these is the area of publication. The Trust, in cooperation with the other cosponsors of this conference, plans to publish the proceedings of this conference for its members as well as for those attending the conference and for those working in positions with code responsibilities that affect preservation.

Field Service Plans

In the area of field services the National Trust serves as a national clearinghouse, receiving an abundance of mail on issues brought to its attention by a rapidly increasing membership. Many of these inquiries relate to code matters. The responses to the survey that was included with registration information for the conference indicated the wide range of preservation issues generated by existing code requirements. This survey is reflective of many of the issues coming to the attention of the Trust. The Department of Field Services hopes to continue to serve as a communication vehicle both in responding to issues coming to its attention and in bringing those issues to the attention of national code organizations. It also hopes to maintain the liaison that has been established during the organizing of this conference.

Education Plans

In the area of education, the National Trust can play an important role by continuing the process of on site consultation, perhaps initially through the expanding effort of the Trust in developing regional offices. To date offices in San Francisco and Chicago have been established and a Boston office serving the New England area is about to open.* Perhaps as an extension of the conference it may be wise to consider the development of smaller, more regionally focused conferences that would bring together state and regional code officials and the state historic preservation officer that now exist in each state as a result of the 1966 National Historic Preservation Act. Through these offices there is now a national network of communication and there is public responsibility for preservation at the state level. In many states the state historic preservation offices are already constructively working with those responsible for state building codes. But in many other states that is not the case.

The National Trust hopes to accept invitations for membership, not only in organizations but on specific committees, that have been extended as a result of the conference (for example, the invitation to become a member of the National Fire Protection Association Committee on Museums, Libraries and Historic Buildings). Perhaps a similar working relationship can be established with the other four major national code groups.

Development of Models

Perhaps properties owned by the National Trust and the many properties owned by member organizations provide an opportunity to consider and determine what special studies need to be undertaken to examine the relative merits of different types of fire protection systems and to study issues relating to the placement of stairways and hardware in buildings. At the tour of Gadsby's Tavern, some of the code officials discussed what the Alexandria, Va., code officials were requiring in the tavern in comparison to what they would allow in their BOCA situation. There is potential here for the development of a series of case studies and models for the application of building codes to historic structures. The Trust would hope to play a catalytic role in publishing the results of such proposed studies so that they too might be used as national models.

Evident at the conference was the pleasure of code officials, architects and preservationists in coming together, airing respective viewpoints and entering into some initial discussions at least on a national level. It is to be hoped that this interchange will continue on a more systematic basis, and the Trust hopes to be able to accept the many invitations for cooperation.

*The New England Field Service Office, jointly sponsored with the Society for the Preservation of New England Antiquities, opened September 11, 1974. — ed.

Summary

The Code Official's View

LEO J. CANTOR, PE

Leo J. Cantor, PE, is commissioner of buildings in Richmond, Va.

These comments are those of an individual building code official and not representative of any agency. A valid comment for inclusion in this summary was given by one of the conference participants: "I think the National Trust should be commended for getting code officials, architects and preservationists together in an amiable atmosphere to discuss an area of mutual interest. Although in daily work effort one would think they were at opposite ends of the world, actually they are all working toward the same objective."

In listening to presentations by professionals in design and in planning, it was apparent that restoration of historic structures is taking place even under current constraints of codes and standards. The problem area is how to execute restorations in the most effective manner without being inhibited by "indiscriminate" interpretation of the building code regulations and standards. Topics discussed by some of the early speakers and then expanded later were the definitions of a historic district and a historic structure. Although it has been stated, it should be emphasized that the establishment of a historic district is not a building code regulation; one is a special land use control and the other is a building construction control. As a building official the author has suggested rectification of the Building Officials and Code Administrators (BOCA) code change by removing from the shoulders of the building official the task of determining the historical nature of any structure.

Adaptive use is the key point in much of the discussion of the conference. When does one draw the line between adaptation and exploitation? Bernard Cabelus made the point in mentioning a person that moved an alleged historic building a mile down the road, claiming historic restoration or preservation motives.

As a building official, the author is literal in interpreting historic preservation and restoration in the exact terms described. For example, the John Marshall House, St. John's Church and the Robert E. Lee residence should be interpreted as restorations. BOCA identifies clearly what a place of assembly is, and the John Marshall House is not a place of assembly. If it were, many restorations would have been "hogtied" long ago. The house museum type of restoration, from a technical building official standpoint, is not called a house museum because it is not a museum according to building code. A museum is a place of assembly, which is defined as having 100 or more occupants.

There are mechanisms within the code that give some latitude to the repair and alteration of buildings that do not undergo a change of occupancy or usage. Of course, if a residential structure is used as a massage parlor code officials will look askance and not consider this a historical restoration. That is facetious, but it is important to get one point clarified: We have to rely on good faith. Certainly the members of the National Trust are not advocating the exploitation of properties. What we are more concerned with is how to preserve the historic ambience while allowing for adaptation of historic buildings for current use.

Section 318.0 of the BOCA code is only a statement recognizing the features of good code practice. Those architects who have dealt with building codes have registered allegations that some local codes are specification oriented and thus do not provide flexibility for the designer. However, model codes for the most part are composed of performance-type regulations whose basic purpose is to state the general requirements for constructing safe buildings. Professionals have to design buildings using those criteria. Section 318.0 essentially implies that once the historical nature of a structure is established by experts and the historic building is being preserved and the work to restore this building is done by certified architects and engineers, those certified have the right to use their resourcefulness and talent to restore and design the building to meet basic tenets of health, safety and welfare without being hampered by some of the restraints that are present in current specific code requirements. Stairways and egress are common problems that are encountered. Some believe that early fire protection systems can overcome these problems. New technology has enabled that, and one can inject new technology into old structures to salvage them from a safety standpoint.

The historic district should be understood as a function of governmental authority that transcends any building code involvement. The historic district is similar to a residential (R-1) zone where only single family buildings can be constructed. The historic district puts a boundary on an area that says buildings now have to conform to visual and aesthetic requirements in harmony with the area. These requirements are difficult to achieve, and perhaps some of them can be challenged constitutionally. More common than the historic district is an identified historic building. The National Register has identified and documented a number of these buildings. Once a building is so identified it is similar to the historic district. Therefore, whatever is necessary to make that building safe should be developed by the professional designer and not be restricted to literal and conventional building code requirements.

The building official should have some of the same professional latitude that architects have. Too many times building officials are stereotyped as bureaucrats. Architects must trust that building officials have the same degree of professionalism as they do. Section 318.0 seems to recognize the harmony of professionalism of the architect and the design engineer and the enlightened building official who is willing to work with the architect and engineer to review and ensure that the building is designed safely. There are now many programs certifying building officials—BOCA is doing this. All the model code groups are now in support of the National Academy of Code Administration (NACA). The National Trust is invited to join BOCA and also to join NACA, which is interested in upgrading the professionalism of code administrators.

Remember, a building official is more accurately described as a code administrator. The main function is to enforce a law. The building official is the agent that the public has chosen to interpose between the public and the owner to ensure that certain laws are being followed. One of those laws requires safe design by a professional who has demonstrated competency to state or local governmental authority when becoming certified as a professional. Building code officials do not hide behind the skirts of certified professional designers. Spot checking and review of basic requirements has to be done by the building official to discover any human error by the designer. It is an extra check and review process, but not one to displace or supplant the responsibilities of the professional.

It would be presumptuous for one building official to presume to have correlated all of the conference comments comprehensively. It is hoped some of the highlights have been discussed.

The Architect's View

NICHOLAS H. HOLMES, JR., AIA

Nicholas H. Holmes, Jr., is senior architect with Holmes & Geer, Architect-Engineer, and specializes in historic restorations. He is a member of the Architectural Review Board of Mobile, Ala., and is a member of the Committee on Historic Resources, American Institute of Architects.

Preservation is not a clearcut or easy problem for the owner, architect, contractor or building official. Once a successful banker in the community commissioned me to assist him in moving an 1840 residence that could not remain on its original site to a rural location by a lovely river to become a community center in a new residential development. There were many problems: The new floor elevation had to meet the requirements of the recently enacted regulations promulgated after the passage of the federal wave-wash insurance program. The building, which had already withstood 130 years of hurricanes, had to have additional reinforcement to withstand the next 130 years of hurricanes; the occupancy would change from residential to assembly, and so forth and so on.

The banker-owner and I ruminated on what contractor in town was deserving of such a job, and the contractor son of the owner was suggested. At first the banker demurred, but architectural logic and my self-preservation won and I was given permission to approach the son. After some of the complexities were outlined to him, he pointed an index finger at his temple, let his hammerlike thumb fall and asked, "How did a nice architect like you get messed up in a thing like this?"

And yet those who have chosen to labor in this rather weedy and overgrown corner of the Lord's vineyard must get cracking. Much was said at the conference regarding the purposes of building codes; protection of life, health and safety has been repeatedly mentioned. But in many areas of the country the codes are rightfully being used to protect other values that are also important to communities for many different reasons: aesthetic reasons, economic reasons and historical reasons.

A wide disparity in viewpoint exists between that of W. I. Kelley, who stated that "methods to make safe yet retain *must* be found," ("New Orleans Historic Preservation and the Building Code," p. 37) and that of Robert E. O'Bannon, who stated that in case of a change of occupancy "the structure should be considered as having characteristics that are a potential threat until a thorough investigation has either vindicated it or confirmed the presence of provable dangers." ("Historic Buildings and the Uniform Building Code," p. 61). This disparity of viewpoint continues even in the language used. Kelley employs in his forensic vocabulary terms such as "buildings of historical nature," whereas O'Bannon poses the rhetorical question, "Just what is a historic building?"

It is not being implied that either one of these gentlemen would be more lax or more stringent than the other in code enforcement. Instead, an attitude engendered by aesthetic, economic and historical factors is being evidenced. New Orleans possesses a citizenry that loves and admires its old buildings and is a city that depends on architectural tourism. It has never—to my knowledge—suffered a damaging earthquake. On the other hand, West Coast cities have other bases for their economies and are constantly worried that the entire region west of the Rockies may slide off into the Pacific.

The most astonishing thing to consider in this comparison is that both of these gentlemen are enforcing the same code. Could they not then be brought closer together in outlook if the Uniform Building Code adopted the proposed amendment, section 318.0, devised by code officials in Virginia? The amendment provides nothing radical; it simply recognizes that certain structures are classified as historic buildings by constituted authorities. It implies that these buildings should be excused from the letter of the code if the design professional can introduce compensating factors that will render the building safe—in the opinion of the enforcement agency. There is nothing in this provision that approaches a blanket waiver for any building, nor would any responsible professional want or seek such a waiver. Building officials in an area fortunate enough to possess a number of historic structures should welcome such a code provision —it gives officials some place to hang their hats!

In addition to the amendment, there is another line of study that should be pursued by code drafters. Orin Bullock has obviously been using this concept for years, whether sanctioned by written law or not, and Karel Yasko has listed it as one of the four GSA elements in fire safety—that is, emergency preparedness.

I once visited a chemical plant in anticipation of work on some of its locker room facilities. Suddenly there was a great eruption of hooters and sirens, and the fire engine, the foam truck, the ambulance and the fire marshal all commenced a grand parade around the plant. The guide said, "If this happens and it ain't 10:00 Tuesday morning—then run like hell for the gate." Fire drills are still common—not only in industry and with the GSA but in every school system in the country. On my way to the conference I was twice told what to do if the aircraft lost pressure and twice again how to get to the emergency doors. Why should not emergency procedures be a regular indoctrination for those who work in any building—historic or not? Mr. Bullock's instructions to fasten back inward-opening doors when a building occupancy changes from residential to assembly is certainly a move in the right direction. To date, no code recognizes the fact that buildings are occupied by human beings who can be instructed in methods of behavior under adverse circumstances.

Murvan Maxwell, W. I. Kelley and Giorgio Cavaglieri have pointed out the advisability of conferring with the building official at a very early stage. I certainly agree. Early consultation is the way to avoid many a stormy passage for all buildings, not just restoration jobs. It can be considered a matter of good manners, but in this, as in most other facets of human behavior these days, good manners seem to be sadly missing.

The sophisticated boards of appeals arrangement now in use in New Orleans is impressive. In many smaller cities this function is handled by the city commission, which means that there is actually no review at all. City commissioners are not competent in this realm; they must either uphold or overrule the chief inspector, and they do not normally possess the knowledge or experience required to intelligently do either. Could not some provision be introduced into all codes delineating technical competency required of persons on any board of appeals or review committee? The chief inspector would probably welcome technical assistance when reviewing new concepts that are being introduced in old buildings.

An interesting idea and a major difference in viewpoint on the question of evaluating the worth of a building was brought out. This is most important when one discusses with a building official the cost of proposed improvements versus the value of the structure—"the percentage." Whereas Richmond uses assessed values, New Orleans uses replacement values.

Consider Gadsby's Tavern in Alexandria, Va. I do not know its assessed value, but I have some idea of its replacement value. How many have bought handmade brick in the last few years, or wide virgin timber flooring, or handcarved mantels or run plaster molds? These items are not lightly or cheaply come by. Some of them, frankly, are irreplaceable. Fifty percent of an assessed value is a figure, but 50 percent of an irreplaceable item is infinity.

Another point made by several speakers had to do with input from the architectural profession. In this I must plead guilty, having never attended a codes conference. The only defense is that I have never been invited to a codes conference, and being a shy and retiring sort of fellow never even thought of asking to attend. But a friend in north Alabama is more brash; he is also a member of the AIA Committee on Historic Resources and is assistant state preservation coordinator for Alabama. Recently he sent a clipping from the house magazine of the Southern Building Code Congress mentioning that the historic preservation amendment (section 318.0) would be considered at its next meeting in Birmingham. Attached was a note, "Dear Nick—Enclosed is a clipping for your information. Would it help if I try to make the Birmingham meeting? Let me know time and place." Well, in spite of my not knowing the time and place and my not having received an engraved invitation, Harvey and I decided to attend. Then when Murvan Maxwell introduces the amendment one of us plans to holler and yell while the other beats the drum.

One element has been mentioned but needs amplification—*why* all this concern and worry and talk? William Murtagh touched on the reason when he attacked the attempt to apply the basic premise of euclidean geometry: that the whole is equal to the sum of its parts. He proved to the author's satisfaction that this is not so and that the whole is greater than the sum of its parts. In this case the "whole" is the whole continuum of our architectural heritage. The archaeologist spends years looking at potsherds and stone tools, trying to learn something of the cultures that developed these artifacts and that finally evolved into our present culture. The buildings of our predecessors are parts of these cultural manifestations. The continuum of our architecture is a vivid, visible reminder of the continuum of our development as a people and a nation. It is all there: the good and the bad, the beautiful, the romantic, the whimsical, the ridiculous, the pretentious and the honest. Its preservation is worth the effort.

The final question for consideration is Where do we go from here? One of the earliest neolithic agricultural peoples is now referred to as the "slashers and burners." They cleared small plots, burned the clearings and then planted their crops. They had no knowledge of fertilizers or concept of replenishing the soil, so after a season or so the soil became sterile and unproductive. But they had unlimited land, so they thought, and they simply moved to a new location and repeated the process. This proved to be a wasteful way to do things and the method was eventually abandoned. And yet how similar it is to our own pattern of living, where each succeeding generation moves to a more fashionable address and leaves behind a decaying neighborhood. In rich, wasteful America the slashers and burners are still evident. An English friend visited our city, Mobile, Ala., recently, toward the end of a cross-country tour and remarked, "You Americans are tearing down permanent buildings and putting up temporary buildings."

But the times are changing. It is not just leadership that is in short supply; we are running out of everything. Last week I received a notice of the annual meeting of the Gulf States Region of the American Institute of Architects, inviting entries in the architectural competition. It was astonishing to read that the subject of the competition was "Recycling of Existing Buildings."

If the architects of this country have finally gotten the word, then the word has gone to the four corners of the earth and bounced back again.

In the course of a tour of Nashville I was shown the Nashville Union Station, Richardson Romanesque, built about 1890 and a preservation problem. Now when I was in school I was taught that those sorts of buildings were horrible examples of eclecticism that should be consigned to outer darkness. But not the new breed of student; three architectural students from the University of Tennessee had been assigned the problem of designing adaptive uses for old Union Station. The problem of adapting old buildings to new uses is not going to go away. It is going to be here from now on, and that is why this is an important conference. We have all gained a better understanding of preservation problems and the knowledge that through cooperation, inventiveness and imagination acceptable solutions can be devised.

Discussion

Comments made by the speakers and the audience during the summary discussion are here summarized.

A lot of good preservation has been done in spite of the laws, but architects have pushed building officials beyond a reasonable point. Officials take a considerable risk when they give permission to lay aside building code regulations; consider what will happen if someone is killed. One discrepancy that is being remedied is the fact the governmental agencies legally are not subject to their own law. However, governmental agencies are becoming increasingly responsive to persons who protest the moral discrepancy of such a legalistic interpretation. These two aspects of the current preservation situation, along with the increased volume of preservation, have resulted in this conference. Preservation through adaptive use is becoming increasingly important; we are becoming saturated with preservation projects that are only museums.

It is assumed that decisions of building code officials on preservation projects have been in harmony with all building code regulations. It is foolish when officials stick their necks out and lay a regulation aside. Wherever construction has been executed, codes should be applied in compliance with the regulations that are embodied within those codes. The only consideration is whether additional flexibility in codes is needed because there has been an increase of historic preservation projects. The establishment of historic districts has now had an additional impact on building codes. What the historic district has done is to establish a new zone. This new zone represents the fact that these buildings are not going to be restored to their historic state. Instead, what is being attempted is not the restoration of a building, but an ambient environment. These buildings become repaired houses rather than old houses, which is really what is causing the problem with building codes.

The question of when an adaptation is not an exploitation must also be considered. Section 318.0 in Virginia attempts to allow a joint action by the government through the building official and the professional involved in a preservation project to see that a building is designed with the proper safeguards. As far as the historical aspect of the building and its adaptation, that will be a function of what the historic district is all about. In other words, limits on adaptation of buildings to any and every use are a function of the historic district legislation, not the building official. Limits cannot be categorically placed on adaptive use as related to the historical significance of a building. There is no absolute point at which the adaptive use is so far removed from the original use that it can no longer be justified. Often, working on a restoration job and not being able to meet code requirements pushes architects toward the impossibility of funding their projects. Certain adaptive uses may push the cost beyond economic practicality.

Some persons believe that the only value of government is to provide cultural continuity. If it came to a final crunch in testing whether cultural continuity or public safety would prevail, I often wonder how it would come down as a final constitutional decision. Would a historic structure be compromised in favor of public safety, or vice versa? Legislation before the U.S. Congress would prevent contractors and owners from writing off the cost of demolishing a building listed in the National Register of Historic Places.

The statewide building code of Virginia requires everyone below the federal government to comply with the code. The local government may violate the zoning ordinance, but it must comply with the building code. If an area is declared a historic district, the building official's jurisdiction does not cease at the periphery of the district. A building official has to receive verification from a local historic district commission that a proposed alteration necessitated by the code meets the aesthetic approval of this commission, which has defined what is significant in that historic district. To make these alterations, architects must design according to the building code requirements in that locality. For example, if the use of the building is changed, the structure must meet the requirements of that new use. What section 318.0 will try to accommodate is what has been happening with the increasing number of historic districts, not subjecting the adaptive use to the total constraints of the building code. 318.0 allows the architect to design resourcefully. A historically insignificant building within a historic district is renovated and redesigned to fit the flavor of the district and is in compliance with the building codes, with the provision that the building can be remodeled with an adaptive use appropriate for the district.

Appendixes

APPENDIX A

Examples of National Code Provisions Relating to Historic Buildings

Basic Building Code of the Building Officials and Code Administrators, International

Section 318.0 Special Historic Buildings and Districts

The provisions of this code, relating to the construction, repair, alteration, enlargement, restoration and moving of buildings or structures shall not be mandatory for existing buildings or structures identified and classified by the building official as Historic Buildings subject to the approval of the Board of Appeals when such buildings are judged by the building official to be safe and in the public's interest of health, safety and welfare regarding any proposed construction, alteration, repair, enlargement, relocation, and location within fire districts. All such approvals must be based on the applicant's complete submission of professional architectural and engineering plans and specifications bearing the professional seal of the designer.

Uniform Building Code of the International Conference of Building Officials

Section 203 (j) Historic Buildings

Repairs, alterations and additions necessary for the preservation, restoration, rehabilitation or continued use of a building or structure may be made without conformance to all of the requirements of this Code, when authorized by the Building Official provided:

1. The building or structure has been designated by official action of the legislative body as having special historical or architectural significance.
2. Any unsafe conditions as described in Section 203, will be corrected in accordance with approved plans.
3. Any substandard conditions will be corrected in accordance with approved plans.
4. The restored building or structure will be less hazardous, based on life and fire risk, than the existing building.

APPENDIX B

Examples of State Code Provisions Relating to Historic Buildings

VIRGINIA UNIFORM STATEWIDE BUILDING CODE, 1974 ACCUMULATIVE SUPPLEMENT

Section 318.0 Special Historic Buildings and Districts

The provisions of the Basic Code, relating to the construction, repair, alteration, enlargement, restoration and moving of buildings or structures shall not be mandatory for existing buildings or structures identified and classified by the State and/or local government authority as Historic Buildings subject to approval of the Review Board when such buildings are judged by the building official to be safe and in the public's interest of health, safety and welfare regarding any proposed construction, alteration, repair, enlargement, relocation, and location within fire districts. All such approvals must be based on the applicant's complete submission of professional architectural and engineering plans and specifications bearing the professional seal of the designer.

STATE OF OREGON STRUCTURAL SPECIALTY CODE AND FIRE AND LIFE SAFETY CODE, 1973 EDITION

Section 409 Definitions

Historical Building: is any building or structure designated under a local government landmark or historic district ordinance, buildings or structures entered in the National Register of Historic Places, buildings or structures listed in the Oregon State Inventory of Historical Sites and Buildings, and properties approved for nomination to the National Register of Historic Places by the State of Oregon Advisory Committee on Historic Preservation.

Section 104 Application to Existing Buildings

(k) Historical Buildings. Buildings or structures designated historical buildings as defined under Section 409 shall not be required to comply with the requirements of this Code for those items approved to be exempted by the Historical Building Review Committee and judged to be in the public interest to the preservation of such buildings.

Section 105 Moved Buildings

Exception: Buildings or structures designated historical buildings as defined under Section 409 and moved as a means for their preservation shall not be required to comply with the requirements of this code for those items approved to be exempted by the Historical Building Review Committee.

Section 204 Board of Appeals

(d) Historical Building Review Committee: In order to determine to what extent historical buildings, defined as such under Section 409, must be made to comply with the requirements of this Code, without destroying the qualities which necessitate the preservation, there is herewith established a statewide Oregon Historical Building Review Committee. This Committee is charged with the responsibility of granting variances for the preservation of designated historical buildings but is not empowered to grant waivers per se, in that the code compliance is one means of preservation. The Review Committee shall consist of the Director of the Department of Commerce, or his representative; the State Fire Marshal, or his representative; the Building Official or local government representative of the municipality in which an historical building is to be reviewed for preservation shall participate in the review process on the Committee at the time a building is to be reviewed in his jurisdiction; and the State of Oregon Preservation Officer or his staff representative; and the Review Committee shall have the power to waive any provision of the combined state building code when in their opinions such historic buildings are not hazardous to life or health and the proposed variance does not conflict with the public interest. In order that a local municipality may be assured that a declared historic building will not be hazardous, they may request that such building be first declared structurally sound by an Oregon licensed engineer or architect and that sufficient plans and specifications be submitted to them, stamped by an Oregon licensed engineer or architect, to insure that such Committee-approved variances will not permit hazardous conditions or be against the public interest. The Committee shall consider both the historic performance of the building and the occupancy classification. Any variances by the Committee shall be subject to the established occupancy classification, and any changes in occupancy classification shall terminate the Committee's approval, subjecting the building or structure to be resubmitted for reapproval or abated. All final Review Committee actions shall be subject to review and final approval by the Structural Codes Advisory Board. The Committee shall adopt reasonable rules and regulations for conducting its business.

Exception: In areas exempted from fire and life safety review under ORS 476 030, the historical building review committee shall be the local Historical Building Review Board of a city or county. If none exists, the board shall be the State Historical Building Review Committee.